IS IT PAINFUL TO THINK?

IS IT PAINFUL TO THINK?

CONVERSATIONS WITH

ARNE NAESS

David Rothenberg

UNIVERSITY OF MINNESOTA PRESS
MINNEAPOLIS   LONDON

Copyright 1993 by the Regents of the University of Minnesota

Published by the University of Minnesota Press
2037 University Avenue Southeast, Minneapolis, MN 55414
Printed in the United States of America on acid-free paper

Design by Susan Gutnik

Library of Congress Cataloging-in-Publication Data

Rothenberg, David, 1962-
    Is it painful to think? : conversations with Arne Naess / David
Rothenberg.
        p.   cm.
    Includes index.
    ISBN 0-8166-2151-9 (alk. paper).—ISBN 0-8166-2152-7 (pbk. :
alk. paper)
    1. Naess, Arne.   2. Philosophers—Norway.   3. Philosophy of nature.
4. Human ecology—Norway—Philosophy.   I. Naess, Arne.
B4445.N344R68   1993
198'.1—dc20   92-12235
                                                                    CIP

SOCRATES: In order not to feel pity for your thirty-year-olds, you must be extremely careful how you introduce them to dialectic. . . . I do not think it has escaped your notice that when youths get their first taste of reasoned discourse they take it as a game and use it to contradict. . . . They delight like puppies in pulling about and tearing with words all who approach them.

GLAUCON: Most true.

SOCRATES: But an older man will not share this craze; he will imitate one who is willing to converse in order to discover the truth rather than one who is merely contradicting for play. He will himself be more deliberate and will bring honor rather than discredit to the pursuit of philosophy.

GLAUCON: Right.

Plato, Republic VII, 539b-d

CONTENTS

PREFACE:
WHY TRUST THE PAIN?

Arne Naess—Norwegian philosopher, deep ecologist, and alpinist extraordinaire—is now eighty years old, and he still tries to avoid doing the same thing twice. The minute you try to pin him down to one viewpoint or another, to one school of thought, or to one style of life, he continues to surprise. Remaining an individual, he is suspicious of any group that would have someone like him for a member—including those who try to take stock of their own lives, turning around and considering the range of experiences and decisions that have made each of us what we are. Only in the last few years, as past and distant memories began to seem more precise and distinct than more recent ones, did he decide that this kind of personal history might be worthy of some attention.

I packed my rucksack and flew to Oslo, took the first train to the Hardangervidda, and started the long walk uphill. We spent ten days in Arne's hut at Tvergastein, rarely seeing the sun. With the views tenuous and the rain heavy, immediate experience faded away as we began to talk about the past. Socked in by clouds, we could have been anywhere, tracing remembrances and events, composing a life through the diverse threads of the twentieth century.

Here is a vision of Arne Naess that his works do not readily reveal: a man restlessly seeking truth through a turbulent century. Here you will not find summaries of his ideas, but the happenings that shaped them. Most of all, what comes through is an attitude, an approach to life that begins in wonder—at the vast possibility the world offers us—and leads to joy in choosing our own way of partaking in this awe, finding our own place, and ensuring that it will be a location meaningful to others and to the world as a whole.

The title asks the question, Is it painful to think? Arne believes that it is, but it is a pain we should not shirk, a suffering we must learn to love the more we engage in it. Society sets us up to be free of this necessary pain, so we need to turn against the rules and question what lies around us. It is not an easy route—this old path toward doubt. Enough philosophers have beckoned us onto it throughout history, but few have had such a good time along it as Arne. For him, life has been something to enjoy completely from the very first moment it filled him with wonder. And no attempt to explain anything should ever forget this amazement at the richness of the world and our unique place within it.

The original tapes were transcribed by Jaime Wolf and Barbara Kantner, with the assistance of Chip Blake and Alison Robb. Thanks to Barbara Coffin, Barbara Dean, and Ole Rikard Høisæther for editorial advice and support throughout the writing process. Kit Fai Naess has helped to select appropriate photographs, and Jørn Siljeholm has carted more than a few packages back and forth between Boston and Oslo. Thanks to Symbiotics, Inc., for donating information services. I am especially grateful for the financial assistance of Arne Naess, Jr., without whom much of this work would not have been possible.

David Rothenberg
Cambridge, Massachusetts
October 1991

INTRODUCTION:
FROM SCIENCE TO THE SELF

*I*n central Norway there is a mountain, Hallingskarvet, a large, long ridge like a huge loaf of bread. Imagine that it rose too fast in the oven, making a sharp cliff on the southern side of the crust. Beneath this precipice stands a tiny hut, at the place called Tvergastein. The rain pelts the cottage walls, and I am sitting inside by the tiny wood stove with Arne Naess, listening to the story of his life.

The basic facts of the man's career are clear enough: After a period of study in Paris, Vienna, and Berkeley, he becomes, at age twenty-seven, the youngest full professor of philosophy in Norway's history. He then begins a quiet revolution in the country's educational system, leading all students to a more reflective form of education that requires them to investigate norms and values. He distinguishes himself as a mountaineer from the Jotunheimen to the Himalaya, and becomes deeply touched by the thought of Spinoza and Gandhi. Because he supports the clandestine resistance against the Nazi occupation, he is later called by UNESCO to define democracy for the world. Following thirty years of professorhood, he opts for early retirement to devote himself to the urgencies of the environmental crisis. After he coins the phrase "deep ecology," his fame spreads across the worldwide ecological vanguard as the spokesman and symbol for a vision of a world in which we protect the environment as a part of ourselves, never in opposition to humanity.

This says a bit about a life as a river of accomplishments, but little about the spirit of the man himself. Mention the name Arne Naess to those who have known him and you will no doubt stir a flurry of controversy. He has amused some and angered others, refusing to be pinned down to one field or one stance. Some say he has never grown up, while others are sure he has been an old man since birth. Some say he has invented a whole Norwegian style in philosophy, while others insist he had a great gift in logic, but threw it to the winds so that he could spend more time climbing.

To get beyond the endless sway of opinion about a person, one must go directly to the source. I first heard of Arne Naess during my college years—there were rumors that on the high Norwegian mountain plateau called the Hardangervidda lived an old, learned philosopher who had quit teaching to save the planet Earth. His story gave some credence to the power of ideas in a world whose attention span was rapidly decreasing. Could a philosopher, an artist of concepts, actually make a difference anymore? I asked him this in an innocent letter, and he sent piles of obscure articles, from "The Case against Science" and "The Place of Joy . . . in a World of Fact" to "Self-Realization in Mixed Communities of Humans, Bears, Sheep, and Wolves." His letter to me ended with the words "We will climb together if you come to Norway."

He was already seventy-one when I got there two years later, and there we were, roped up on the crumbling cliffs of Hallings-karvet. He muttered something about hoping I was a better thinker than climber, all the while kicking gravel in my face from above as a kind of intimidation. Nonetheless, he ended by asking me if I would like to stay there a bit longer. Altogether, I spent just under two years in Oslo, researching the Norwegian tradition of nature philosophy and gradually letting my own perspective germinate out of the ambiguous seeds he had planted.

I returned in the summer of 1990 specifically to query Arne on the events and tendencies of his long and varied life. So these are the conversations of two friends who have known each other for at least a few years, one exactly fifty years older than the other. We are retracing ground familiar to both of us, and so the story, though clear, may require some introduction. The following are moments from the history of his work—not a complete account, but episodes from what has mattered most to him.

What I am after here is the spirit of the man—the mischievous troublemaker always at a distance from each position he espouses. This is a restless and skeptical questioner, who is always jumping from theme to position, challenging the established dogmas with a gentle irreverence that does not preclude respect. His own revelations from childhood in chapter 1 do much to explain the basic theme of his lifetime stance: distance from the people and conventions around him. Always a committed outsider, Arne empathizes with such far-away languages as Sanskrit and remote organisms (sandfleas, for example). The near and familiar are much harder for him to touch.

Yet, when in Vienna in the thirties and caught up in the movement to bring philosophy back to the mores and expressions of "common sense," it was only Arne Naess who wondered just how the philosopher should go about finding out what the "common" conception is:

> Between the exponents of the different "opinions of truth" great controversies are set afoot. N holds that the standpoint of M is "untenable," . . . "In conflict with the timeless laws of reason," or "typical of Yankees." The individual philosophers put forth their theories without much hesitation as "the solution of the problem." . . . The discussion has already lasted some 2500 years.

The quotation is from one of Arne's earliest works, *"Truth" as Conceived by Those Who Are Not Professional Philosophers* (1939). So it's common sense that you want? Well, then, go ask people on the street what they think about "truth." He used questionnaires, the emerging tool of the newly empirical social sciences, to find out what "common" people really thought. The resulting tome was spurned by academic orthodoxy as being mere sociology, nothing worthy of as lofty a field as philosophy. And yet, shouldn't the sense that is common to all come from all types of people, from all walks of life? What better method than to go out into the field and ask everyone one meets what they think the word "truth" means? Written and oral answers were collected. The interviews at times resemble a drama somewhere between Ibsen and Beckett:

> Subject #79, a student of medicine, twenty-two years old.
>
> NAESS: Give me an example of something that is true.
>
> 79: No, I do not think I understand any of this.
>
> NAESS: Do you use the word "true" now and then?
>
> 79: (The subject looks rather unhappy.) I believe I am a bad subject.
>
> NAESS: Have you had your breakfast today?
>
> 79: Yes.
>
> NAESS: It is true?
>
> 79: Yes.
>
> NAESS: Are there some trees out there?
>
> 79: I cannot understand what you are aiming at.
>
> NAESS: Examples of what is true, as I have explained it.
>
> 79: Miss Jonsen is engaged—in any case, she has been engaged.
>
> NAESS: More.
>
> 79: Is it true that there has been rat-typhoid here?
>
> NAESS: Not in the form of questions.
>
> 79: It is true that there has been rat-typhoid here.

Nothing is as complicated as the truth. (You will see enough of this kind of dialogue between Arne Naess and me in the pages that follow. The inquiry yearns for precision, while responses remain elusive. The answer comes out in the rhythm of the story.) There was no single empirically deduced "common sense"—the answers covered the spectrum of philosophical viewpoints from throughout the history of possible ideas of what truth is: Comparing the explicit and implicit views of amateur and professional philosophers on the difficulties in question, Arne found no serious differences.

Inconclusive, you say? It is often said of philosophy that its questions matter more than its answers. This may be why the same debates go on for two and a half millennia without any demonstrable progress. In fact, as Arne will relate much later, any sufficiently protracted series of questions will lead the inquisitive person rapidly into philosophy: "Fire up the stove!"—I demand. "Why?"—retorts Arne. "I want some tea." "Why?" "I'm thirsty." "Why?" "Living beings need water." "Why?" "To stay alive." "Why?" "Staying alive is necessary for our survival." "Why survive?" Now, we are into philosophy. And there is no way out.

The young Arne Naess, impressed by the precisions of science, wanted the answers to questions such as these to be testable by experiment. This led him to the psychology laboratories of the University of California, where he became enamored with the rat. Yet, the psychologist who pores over rats adrift in their races and mazes will never really know what the animals want or are thinking. Arne watched them make choices and sift through possibilities—which way to jump, which track to take? He soon decided it was more interesting to watch the scientists who were watching the rats! After all, what could the outsider really know of the rats' thought processes? All the observer notes is the behavior of the investigator, not the reason for the investigation. (Though at least, to the scientist, the philosopher might ask the question, Just why do you do the things you do?)

This kind of behavioral stance was really an early attempt to take the environment as a subject for study. We do not know the workings of rats or of humans, but we can see how they live, measuring the marks they leave on their surrounding world. The rat runs and runs through the maze, a little bit faster each time. And people wreak havoc on the planet Earth. Are we any closer to determining the reason?

Although the behavioral approach draws attention to the problems, it denies the importance of these questions. Plagued by the unanswerables, Arne moved away from the empirical, instead coming to believe it is the observations that are tested by the theories, rather than the reverse. Science tends to wish there were one answer, rather than the innumerable many; but the world outside science desperately needs to be voiced:

A monolithic, soul-shrinking jargon still prevails in discussions on worldviews among creative scientists: it is as if the
prestige of science as a truth-seeking project depended on
the emergence of one definite world picture, the scientific
world picture, as opposed to all the unscientific ones—the
confused, vague, irresponsible metaphysical views, the grand
illusions of the religious believer and of the cognitively irrelevant artist. Increase in uniformity of opinion is cheered as
if it were a reliable indicator of increase in truth content,
neglecting the possibility that it is the urge to conform
which is in operation.

If the practice of science cannot handle the important reaches of
human experience, then Arne Naess has to bid it farewell. The
quote is from *The Pluralist and Possibilist Aspect of the Scientific
Enterprise* (1972), a later work that is the culmination of Naess's
articulation of an alternative to the unification dream of science.
He coined the term "possibilism" to refer to a kind of enlight-
ened skepticism—it's not that all truth need be doubted, but that
anything might happen! No need to have any absolute faith in
causality, and we should always be ready for the pull of the
unknown. What is later described as the valuable diversity of
nature begins for Arne as the vast realm of human alternatives.
We have so many choices as we live in this world, and we should
never forget the multitude of pathways open to us at any time.
There is never just one possible world with which we must make
do—the best of worlds is the one with the most possibilities,
where we learn to see as many as we can.

One would get lost in such a life if one tried to follow each
path every which way. There needs to be some force to guide the
journey, even if it will not be the monolithic truth desired by science. Action demands choice, and Naess believes that we always
act as if we possessed a total view—that is, an implicit vision of
how we fit into the world. It may be the philosopher's job to
describe such a structure, but all of us act as if we have one. The
problem is that if we try to explain just what we believe, what
justifies our actions, the system will always be full of holes.

This is the inadequacy that plagued another Scandinavian
thinker, Søren Kierkegaard, a hundred or more years before
Naess. His answer was successively higher levels of belief, moving

away from the autonomy of the individual self by surrendering freedom to the forgiving benevolence of religion. Arne, however, is not ready to give up any amount of freedom. Instead, he imagines the individual self as something to be realized outward into the world, such that it is enlarged and deepened the more universal experience it is able to contain. He derives this idea not from the abstract shelves of philosophy, but from the committed nonviolent actions of Mohandas Gandhi, who labored to set his nation free. In *Gandhi and Group Conflict* (1974), Naess writes:

> The rock-bottom foundation of the technique for achieving the power of nonviolence is belief in the essential oneness of all life. . . . More than a few people, from their earliest youth, feel a basic unity with and of all the human beings they encounter, a unity that overrides all the differences and makes these appear superficial. Gandhi was one of those fortunate people. [He wrote:] "A drop torn from the ocean perishes without doing any good. If it remains a part of the ocean, it shares the glory of carrying on its bosom a fleet of mighty ships."

Gandhi identified with all the humanity he saw around him, so that he struggled for his own self-realization only in concert with theirs. As the conversations reveal, Arne often experiences people as faraway and elusive, but it is *all* life forms that he chooses to identify with. Thus, his own realization is intimately connected to the realization of all the many living selves that surround him.

Arne speaks of the small "self" and the "Self" with a capital s. The latter is the great Self, which is as near as he will come to the mention of God. It is the unity of the natural world, a singular thing with which we are meant to identify, as when we suddenly feel the suffering of the earth as a whole, under the vast weight of human transformation. And Self-realization is a way to link this intuition of the unity of life with our own individual lives and pursuits. Abraham Maslow thought that one of the criteria for true self-realization was independence from one's environment. But for Naess's Self-realization, it is exactly the opposite. One approaches fulfillment through empathy with the world beyond the ego. This expansion of concern does not diminish humanity, but enriches us by pushing the meaning of humanity further and further away from any one person's interest. As Spinoza says, we approach perfection the more connections we apprehend of the innumerable links and branches that hold the world together as one.

The Norwegian term is *Selv-realisering:* Self-realizing, an activity, not a place one could reach. We cannot get there without taking the rest of the world with us—the Buddhist bodhisattva always returns to earth to help others on their way, and thus never visits Nirvana. The image of a perfect destination is necessary only for us to live out our lives. Like the total view, it is an essential fiction.

This imperative toward care is quite a contrast to Naess's earlier project of the "scientification" of philosophy. The differences appear most poignantly in the real conflicts that he had to live through. Arne initially considered the German invasion of Norway near the beginning of World War II to be nothing remarkable, nothing that should interrupt the single-minded purity of research. But soon, he became annoyed, not by the occupation government, but by the rash and imprecise way Norwegians tended to talk about the enemy—generally complaining, not thinking enough about what they were saying. He still wanted logic to prevail in the understanding of the most emotional constraints of war. The issue of whether the students should go on strike was immediately turned into an example of the tools of logical debate:

Thesis: Students should strike.

Antithesis: Students should not strike.

Pro:
   P_1: A strike would strengthen the home front.
   P_2: The reputation of students, and indirectly of all intellectuals, will suffer a blow if they fail to show solidarity in time of war.
   P_3: A strike should effectively obstruct enemy propaganda by showing that cultural institutions cannot be preserved in an occupied country. . . .

Con:
   C_1: It is to the enemy's advantage if we strike, for then

they can disperse the students who, thus weakened, will be unable to voice their opinions effectively.

C_2: If there is a strike, the enemy will take over all scientific institutions.

C_3: It will be to our country's detriment to have a shortage of graduates when peace comes. . . .

The court was soon moot, since the Germans surrounded the University of Oslo and exported many of the students to concentration camps (where they fared better than many others because they were deemed as Aryan as anyone). In chapter 6 you will read of Naess's role in trying to avert this attack, and will see how he accepted his role of warner.

After the Nazi surrender and the fall of Quisling, Naess started an effort to get the traitors who had cooperated with the enemy to face the families of those they had tortured and often killed. Although the experience was painful in the extreme, it brought with it a kind of absolute resolution to the unfinished stories of soldiers' suffering. There is a way to connect logic to compassion: Make one's effort to care precise and directed in explicit ways. There are things about which one must remain silent, and these are the darkest sides of human possibility, which cannot be hidden and should never be denied.

Still, logic does intrude upon passion. The challenge for each of us is to find the arena in life where we can as individuals best combine them. For Arne, the synthesis that overcomes restlessness came at last with his decision in the sixties to quit his professorship and join the worldwide environmental movement. Here is a grave concern that has brought hundreds to worry and despondency. Many say they love nature, but few can explain why or how to convince those who dissent. This is where the philosopher can help. He may ask, Can the world always seem as if it is about to end, or are we particularly poised on the brink, charged with the decision of whether to respect the earth or overrun it?

Much has been written of Arne Naess as the founder of "deep ecology," a thoughtful approach to environmental problems that looks for its roots deep in the structure of our society and our worldview. I hope to show that this latest interest of his is not a complete about-face from what has come before, but an extension that further hones his character toward Self-realization. The idea of deep ecology should appear deeper if it is understood as flowing out of empiricism, logic, possibilism, and Gandhism, as they have been put to use in deliberation over one of the central issues of our time.

Although it was not until the sixties that the ecology movement was large enough to merit a name, deep sensitivity to nature is for Arne the articulation of something that every child would understand. In reminiscences of his own childhood, we will see unusually sharp recollection of the fascination with the surging stream of life that surrounds us, from the boy transfixed for hours by ocean tide pools, to the youth obsessed with cutting holes in his tent so that he will be able to gaze upon the mountains even while he sleeps. Children all trust and wonder at nature, so it may be something we can all recollect if we delve deeply enough into our formative memories.

Children learn to accept the world by feeling that they have a place within it. There is no vision of home without one's own necessity. If we see the world as enriched because we are looking at it, we will not destroy what we see. This "gestalt view" of humanity's place in nature reinforces a deep ecological mentality, as chapter 8 will investigate. The gestalt perception of nature, which includes our gaze, is also a part of a total view inspired by Spinoza, who wrote in the seventeenth century that the more we know our own connections to the world, the more we know of that world itself. So knowledge of the deepest kind should bind humanity to nature, and not push us further away from the tactile object of its study.

At the same time, deep ecology is a tool of analysis that teaches us to ask more questions to get to the roots of environmental problems; these problems appear as symptoms of fundamental inadequacies of our culture, which has refused to take a clear stand on the vast importance of the natural world for human fulfillment. Here, Arne has built on his training as a philosopher of logic and language, demanding that environmentalists define such slippery terms as "sustainability," "benefit," and "cost." Through philosophical training, one's own position is more firmly grounded in values and norms for action, while training in articulation helps one argue with opponents of ecology.

Deep ecology, then, becomes a political movement whose tenets are described further in the introduction to chapter 7. There is a platform on which adherents are meant to agree, allowing those with very different backgrounds and orientations to rally around a common cause for consensus and then action. The point is to transform society to respect the intrinsic value of nature, and to encourage cultural and biological diversity in the resulting world. As someone who has fought "soul-shrinking monolithic jargon" all his life, Arne will be sure that his ideal society will allow for a vast array of possible human and animal paths. With all living beings enjoying inherent value, worth in themselves, individuality must be cherished as well.

As I read passages of this book of dialogues to the people around me, they often stop me and ask, Is this man serious?—not because any of his ideas seem so outlandish, but because he seems to be having such a good time reviewing the wide and rocky range of arts and sciences he has explored in his life of study. He reminds us again and again that these are desperate times, with the human species at the end of its tether. The future might not resemble the past. Arne reiterates his avowed skepticism, which works both ways: "Anything may happen. Thus, there is always reason to hope." Human life is an avenue toward joy, a joy as much in us as it is in the world. That is always a positive message. Even the smallest possibility for achieving wisdom is reason enough to smile.

The pieces I have composed from the tape recordings of my conversations with Arne Naess cannot hope to convey the completeness of a life so multifarious. Plato did not have such magnetic technology to aid him in the recollection of his friend and mouthpiece, Socrates. (In that example, it was Socrates who asked most of the questions, without leaving much room for response.) I have tried to break through the wall of machinery to recover some of the eternal spirit of the dialogue as philosophical form, allowing the discipline of deep questioning to be coaxed into being through dramatic call and response.

Pay as much attention to what Arne does not mention as to what he says. Notice the way certain tough questions are handled, and decide for yourself which answers seem satisfactory or complete. Although the play may not be performed again, it was improvised once. In the midst of it, I was often reminded of those passages in Plato where the impetuous youth demands answers from the venerable sage, only to be told after a long discussion that he should know them already. The thirty-year-old is usually distraught when the eighty-year-old drifts on to another topic. But that's the way it is. In his own writing, Arne Naess would rather be cautious than complete, to the point of sometimes angering the reader impatient with all the qualification. When he speaks, he does not have such opportunity. With this extended conversation, during one long and gray week in the mountains, we hope for a direct window into the science of the self.

I: CHILDHOOD AND THE DISTANCE

*W*e begin with the ever hazy and essential theme of childhood memories, searching for the roots of lifelong obses-
sions and directions in the image of a precocious and inquisitive
boy, feeling most himself when he is totally alone. How does one
choose the vocation of philosopher, most impractical and most
abstract of sciences, where the questions seem unanswerable and
progress appears to be anathema? In the mountains, of course —
where land and ideas have no limit, and one's own gaze frames
but does not change the glorious world. Every summit looks different, but they are all connected to the same ridges. Each stone
looks different, and that is why the little boy must collect as
many as possible. In his earliest years, Arne began to appreciate
the diversity of nature, where he found a purity so impossible in
the confusing world of other people.

Arne Naess was born into a wealthy Bergen family, the unexpected last child of four. His father died less than a year after he
was born, and his mother, Christine, hired a governess to take
care of the little one. The relationship between mother and son
remained strained, and young Arne developed an aversion to his
mother's love of language and emotional exaggeration. The
theme of distance begins, and the boy finds himself happier with
things than with people. Later, in psychoanalysis in Vienna, he is
told he was searching for his father. Where? In the comfort of
loneliness, in the advice of his older brothers? Most likely in the
mountain itself, silently smiling from above. Ever beckoning to

the climber, but never with any certain embrace. Watching from above, accessible, but only at a distance. Here we see Arne beginning in philosophy, beginning in music, learning to climb, beginning to make friends. But in each enterprise, he remains far away.

Tiny Things, No Pictures

DR: There is one thing I remember most from stories of your childhood. You have said you were immediately attracted to tiny, tiny things in nature. You would go out and look at small living things and gravitate toward them.

AN: Yes. Sure. In chemistry, when I was a boy, it was enough for me to fancy what was going on when one or two drops were put into another liquid, and when I then read about other experiments in the book, I had these drops in mind, colors and so on.

DR: What did you see inside the drops?

AN: Inside the drops! I don't know what I was seeing, but there were fantastic things happening in even one drop. It spread out and, even with two liquids with no colors, they would flow together and spread in fantastic shapes!

Very early, when I was five years old, I was taken to Ustaoset, and somehow, without talking about it, I grasped the concept of freedom, up there, because there were no borders. I could go anywhere and there was no limitation to what I could do. That is when I first saw *this* mountain, Hallingskarvet.

DR: Who took you up here?

AN: My mother. Because my father was one of the first who had a kind of hut here in the mountains. He was among the first to ski over the Hardangervidda.

DR: Is it still here, this hut?

AN: No. Gone. It was very tiny. My mother and my two brothers, we were there and there were others having lots of fun with me. There was a very hard wind and they made me stand like this and they could see that I could be drawn upward because of the wind. And then, of course, I had to be tough.

I don't think I got any idea of what to study from the mountains. I don't think so. But it was here that I learned to appreciate anything that had to do with living beings and minerals and stones. Stones were important . . . collecting stones. I wanted many stones—there should be smallness and also quantity.

DR: Quantity or quality?

AN: Quantity made an impression. I wanted a long, long, long line of small stones.

DR: What did you look for in each stone?

AN: A place in the manifold—that is to say, diversity, infinite diversity.

DR: You were impressed that every one was a little different.

AN: Yes, they all were different. Impossible to describe . . .

DR: Why are little things impressive to you?

AN: Happily, I have written a little psychology of this, that people who later get to be intellectual are often obsessed with tiny details. We have just as strong an experience of the tiny as of the gigantic.

DR: Just as strong, or stronger?

AN: For me, it is stronger. The tiny has always been fascinating. For instance, now because of the dryness, et cetera, this *Gentiana nivalis* outside our window is the most beautiful of the alpine flowers.

DR: Arctic gentian?

AN: Yes. They are extremely small this year because of the dryness. I don't know what else could have done it, but they are rarely more than two centimeters, even when flowering. It makes such a tremendous impression on me: the smallness of it—why, why? It has to do with this old theme in philosophy: microcosm and macrocosm. There are bigger worlds like the stars and the cosmos and then there are smaller worlds, without limits, so to say, and you get just as much complexity and variety in the micro as the macro. But why?

One personal thing must be identified with this tininess: My brothers and sister were much older than I, and I felt small and left alone.

DR: Pascal wrote that humanity is in between the two infinities—the microcosm and the macrocosm.

AN: Yes, and the microcosm for me is identified with one early memory: When I was three years old, my governess was taken away.

The Governess and the Flies

DR: Taken away?

AN: Yes. (Sigh) Mina was her name. Yes. Let's see, I was completely unexpected . . . that my mother should have another child, number six! It was not a glad tiding that I was born.

DR: Number six? But you have only two brothers and one sister.

AN: Yes. Two were already dead. Died when they were two or three years old.

DR: Ah. So how old was your mother, then?

AN: Forty years old. Or more. She was a frustrated woman. And she got this number six, and she had a lot of worries about the two brothers, who were rather wild. She was ill when I was born. She already had Mina to help her. Mina probably fell in love with me. And she tried to satisfy every wish I had, and I had many wishes. For instance, according to my brother, in order to be washed in the bathtub, I had to have at least one fly, dead or alive, I don't know, and she had then to catch a fly. That must not have been in the middle of the winter . . .

DR: You had to have it yourself or it had to be in the room?

AN: It had to be in the water.

DR: In the water, dead?

AN: Yes.

DR: It wouldn't be alive there.

AN: No. Not for long.

DR: So you wanted your governess to kill a fly for you?

AN: To kill it or catch it and put it into the water. Probably not kill it, but put it into the water and it would die by itself. And my mother said that Mina was already beyond fifty and it was touching to see her climb around to catch the fly.

I also liked to have a lot of bottles and pour water into one and then another and see how far up the water would go. In a very broad bottle it would disappear, so to say, and in a long, tall bottle it would go all the way to the top. Piaget has studied how children learn to understand the constancy of fluids. They usually prefer tall bottles . . .

Once when we were going to Nordheimsund, in Hardanger-fjord, we were at the train station. When we were boarding the train, my mother discovered one trunk too many. There were five of us, so we had a lot of trunks. But there was one trunk extra. . . . "What's this?" she asked. And Mina said, "They are bottles for Arne. Arne shall have bottles."

DR: Tall, thin bottles?

AN: Any kind. *The differences are what mattered.* Piaget thought that children liked the tall ones best. But I had to have a lot of different kinds, a suitcase full of bottles. Mina's explanation — "Arne shall have bottles" — was almost a natural law; there was no question of leaving the bottles behind.

DR: So you always had what you needed.

AN: More than that. What I wished, and so I fancied that I also had a lot of power — until she left. Really. I had one human being who was trying to comply with all my wishes.

DR: But she left when you were three.

AN: Yes, because my mother found out that she was spoiling me too much, spoiling me completely. So she was dismissed. There might have been other reasons, but that was certainly one of them. And I didn't get any substitute at all, because my mother had these two other boys and so on. She wouldn't comply with any special wishes of mine, so I got fed up with her. I did not accept my mother.

The Shell against My Mother

DR: Now, what had happened to your father at this point?

AN: He died when I was less than one year old. He got cancer, and my mother went to Germany, and he was in hospital a long time. I was just a small baby and Mina was like a mother to me. I got milk from her.

DR: So you don't remember him much?

AN: No! And later, in psychoanalysis in Vienna, we tried and tried to get some kind of memory of what happened when I was two and three years old. Impossible. All I know is that I didn't accept my mother.

DR: You didn't accept her at all?

AN: No. And so we had to find a reason why. This influenced my life very much, of course. She was a talented, desperate woman, who could have been perhaps an actress. Or a dramatist. She wrote a little play, but one could see which members of the family she was really speaking about, so it was a scandal when it was published. My negative attitude was later directed toward her way of using language, and soon I saw she was acting a lot and was completely unreliable, with much overstatement and emotional hysteria.

DR: So were you resistant to emotion at this time?

AN: Yes. I adopted a tremendous resistance to emotion. When I should be spanked, for instance, normally I should have been carried off to the second floor, or dragged off to a sofa, but when spanking was on the program, I went by myself up the stairs to the second floor, and lay down on the couch to await my fate. I tried to have no reactions before, during, and after, and this was terrible for my mother. When she scolded me, I was just bleak and I would not talk to her for a long while. She was trying to connect with me, and I had some feeling of power over her because I would resist her. Later, this led me to place an enormous weight on impartiality. I tended to use language in a bureaucratic or scientific way, valuing so-called objectivity . . .

DR: You call those the same—bureaucratic and scientific?

AN: Well, when at school when I was supposed to write essays, they came out in a bureaucratic style—no metaphors, whatever I was talking about. You see, this has a basis in the wish that I should not be like my mother . . . I should be the opposite of my mother. . . .

DR: So the stance against emotion is itself emotional?

AN: Oh, yes, very much so. And there you get the possibility for distance . . . I could keep her at a distance, I could keep pain at a distance—being spanked was nothing.

DR: So you craved this distance as you grew older?

AN: I could manipulate and control. Therefore, I developed what is called, in Freudian terms, *Panzercharakter*. That is to say, you have a kind of *Panzer*, a shell. Deep inside, far beneath the shell, is where I lay. You could penetrate to a certain extent, but then it gets tougher and tougher to get in, and you never get completely inside.

DR: So you think you haven't, even now, gotten completely inside . . . ?

AN: No, and of course what arrested development is that I became *Liebesverlust*, lovelorn, when Mina disappeared. And I would defend myself against any other loss. If you don't let anyone completely inside, then you cannot get panicky and crazy for lack of love.

DR: You felt already at the age of three that this one person had gotten close to you and now, no more.

AN: No more of that, because we lose it and then the world is a completely other kind of world without this surrounding warmth. My oldest brother, Ragnar, had some of this, but he disappeared to America when I was eight. His voice was not trembling, but it was a very caressing voice, and he also played on the piano some very romantic things like the Second Movement of the Moonlight Sonata by Spinoza . . .

DR: Beethoven, not Spinoza.

AN: Of course. So you see, this distance helped with scientific clarity. You need objectivity if you are to be a scholar, and you have this single-mindedness to carry you through elaborate tasks. If you are fairly resistant to pain and inconvenience, you can do things with greater force and penetration than a child who has really had a happy childhood, who is just letting all emotions out.

DR: So you believe that with this distance comes a kind of skill—it's easier to accomplish things?

AN: Yes. And this is probably the most difficult thing in living with me for others to accept.

DR: Now, or then?

AN: Always. I am what they call "far away." Again and again, especially the opposite sex will complain, "You are so far away, where are you?" Or "*Was ist es?* What is the matter?" I liked very much to be far away. When I rode in a train from Oslo to Vienna, a very slow train, I could sit and be completely alone. We were, let's say, eight persons in a small compartment, and I would read and write, completely oblivious to the others.

DR: You are always writing something.

AN: Either writing or just thinking. And then I remember once, I was thinking and a woman sitting opposite said, "Please don't stare at me." And I hadn't seen her! She didn't see that my eyes were completely vacant. And even now, my wife, Kit Fai, complains, saying, "You don't really look at me."

DR: You don't, really?

AN: No. And certainly I am often far away. But, of course, this brings a kind of power for concentration. I enter my imagination, but not the poetic imagination.

Poetry and Accuracy

DR: Never poetic? How would you separate the imagination from the poetic? Why is there a sudden distinction?

AN: I had something against any kind of sentiment, as it suggested my mother. I wanted no sentimentality at all. Feelings, yes, strong feelings, but no sentimentality, and most poetry is sentimental, stressing the words themselves.

DR: And you always wanted to go beyond the words . . .

AN: Absolutely. My favorite teacher, Andreas Winsnes—when we were studying Ibsen, he knew that I could have a lot of things to say about thoughts, what was really going on in the drama and what the meaning could be. In class, when he asked, "Now, Naess, read," he would always stop me at once, because I couldn't read with any kind of sentiment. I couldn't quote anything. I was very bad. No quotations at all. I tried to get rid of the words.

DR: Do you remember any of these specific Ibsen tales whose words you wanted to transcend?

AN: *Brand*. Brand was central. I had the same feeling that Brand got—that life must be used for something. For Brand, it was that you should honor God. That was not for me, but without using life for something, it would not be worth living.

DR: Life doesn't have value in itself?

AN: No.

DR: Any kind of life, or just human life?

AN: Human life. It's humans who make the distinction between living for something and just living. . . . So I wouldn't think to apply this to animals.

DR: Were you always oriented toward getting things done, looking for objects as the testament of accomplishment? Would you say, "I've got to write, I've got to read," looking toward specific goals?

AN: Not always. Dreaming also has a place.

DR: To dream is enough . . . ?

AN: I admitted to myself that I could dream, but when I was a student, I was against dreaming, because I saw I could dream a connection between premises and conclusions: I dreamed I solved a philosophic problem that I read about. When I wrote some of it down the next day, I found that the conclusion didn't follow from the premises. This was a terrible discovery.

DR: Is it right to say that at this time, you spent a lot of time by yourself, reading everything you could get your hands on, all kinds of different subjects?

AN: Yes. When I was eleven, I started studying with my older brother Erling. In order to be together with Erling, I had to be quite quiet in his study, and it was natural for me to look up books and those were without illustrations, except diagrams and curves. It was not difficult for me—never mind if it was a foreign language, never mind if it was written in a bureaucratic style. My Norwegian teacher, Winsnes, who was also a philosopher, never gave me a better mark than "fair." A kind of OK mark, not especially high. I myself thought that I had a lot of very fine argumentation, but he also paid attention to the language. It was terrible. The orthography was too old-fashioned.

DR: You were reading Erling's books on economics?

AN: Yes . . .

DR: I have in my hands an economics textbook, four volumes, bought by Arne Naess when he was sixteen years old. This is the sort of thing you were studying in your high school years, and there are minute notes in the margins, in an adolescent kind of handwriting, even a little note paper that says, "What is economics?" with various people's points of view on this.

AN: . . . And this first volume has 549 pages, and the others are the same. But only in this first volume are completely abstract subjects, such as the study of values, Marx, and socialism, treated very carefully, but rather critically, and that had a tremendous influence on my political views. Never mind, I concentrated more and more on the first volume, because the references there are to philosophers.

DR: So this was the beginning? You started from economics value theories and then thought that philosophy might be your true area?

AN: Yes. I then bought this book here by Harald Høffding [*Filosofiens Historie*]. This was my favorite book, two volumes. A very charming history of philosophy. It's from 1894. In Danish. Of course, I got the wrong kind of language from it. There I found Spinoza. At least this philosophy really questioned life itself.

DR: Here it says in bright green ink, scrawled in the margin, "Pay attention to Spinoza's teachings on the endless attributes of God." So already you were picking out things on the manifold diversity.

AN: I recall that a certain Norwegian supreme court member in the Jotunheimen mountains talked with enthusiasm about Spinoza, so although I was completely uninterested in Latin in school, I became excited about Spinoza in Latin. I then got the *Ethics* as a boy . . . Which text I had, I don't know. The Latin of Spinoza is extremely simple, compared to Cicero. Cicero was like my mother, always overstating and using tricks.

DR: You were always suspicious of rhetoric. So you began to decide in high school to drift toward philosophy. You were discovering what it was, and this is what you wanted most to pursue.

The Condition of Music

DR: And what about music at this time?

AN: Well, I was studying piano with Erling Westher when I was fourteen to sixteen years old, and he was a tremendously nice person. I came there after school and very often stayed with him the rest of the day. There was talk of whether I should be a pianist. I spent many hours listening to him and helped to criticize his other students. I was relentless in my commentary.

DR: What about the criticism of emotion and feeling in the music?

AN: There I was somehow very lenient. One could express feelings in music and be lyrical. I was supposed to be good in lyricism.

DR: You were good, so despite your preference for the abstract, you found you could express yourself in music. Do you still find it easier to express emotions in music than in language?

AN: Yes. It doesn't say anything. The meaningfulness is more perfect and complete than language could ever be. Overstatement rarely succeeds. You can, of course, make a caricature of Chopin, though. An immense *ritardando* . . . a fantastic *ritardando*. You have some of the same pitfalls in music as you have in rhetoric.

DR: Some people find in Bach, for example, a more perfect meaning, because it's more clearly structured, rather than a music that depends on emotional statement. Some would say Brahms is overstated.

AN: Yes. I agree. I could always state things in music in the sense of bravura—the opening of Liszt's concerto, I would play the first strokes with enormous gusto, you see, and have a kind of *Übermensch* feeling like Nietzsche . . . It is a gigantism or it is a kind of megalomania, which I could permit myself in music to some extent, but I would then immediately say, "This is not very good, this is not profound, this is abominable in a sense, but, my God! It's nice. My God! It's lustful!"

DR: Did you like to perform for people?

AN: No, never—because I got from my music teacher in Norway a professional sense of criticism. I would criticize his own best pupils. I could see how badly I played compared to how I would like to play. And that's a terrible thing, because then I lost a big joy in life, namely to sit and play as an amateur. I lost that very early.

DR: You don't think you could get it back now, like your brother Ragnar, who at the age of ninety plays the piano many hours a day?

AN: Yes, I think so, but not like my brother. I saw my brother long enough playing the big piano, the Steinway. I sat under it when I was a very tiny boy and I got this impression of complete fullness of meaning — which reinforced my skepticism of language.

DR: It was important for you for meaning to be complete?

AN: Yes. And pure. No doubt, no ambiguity. Precision. Musical thoughts can be more or less clearly expressed, and when criticizing all those students with my teacher, I often said, "Here you disrupted the line." When there was a certain move that clearly departed from what was happening at a certain definite moment, the further away you move, the more clever you must be in order to make it whole. So I was very suspicious when there was any change in the shape of the musical line, whereas my teacher, Westher, was a kind of poet, he saw color in music, he could envision a chord. . . . "This one," and he would look at me and say, "Ha, ha, strange thing, this one. You see, blue. Yellow."

DR: And you didn't hear it that way?

AN: I tried to. I was impressed with his colors . . . impressive, very impressive. There could be hundreds of colors just by changing a little here and there. But that was his specialty. My specialty was structure.

DR: Did you wish, as Goethe said about all arts, that philosophy could aspire to the condition of music?

AN: Of course.

DR: Always?

AN: Yes. And that was tremendously frustrating.

DR: Did you try?

AN: Yes. And then I was moving toward scientific philosophy and that brought on an impasse. But now I think we should eat a little . . .

First Ascents: Friends and Mountains

DR: It is clear that climbing has been one of the most important influences in your life and thoughts. How did you begin?

AN: I was born in a dining room in a very big house, with a still-bigger garden. In a suburb of Oslo, Holmenkollen, known for the ski jump. It was called a garden, but it was not: Three-quarters of it was completely wild, free nature, with big trees and small trees and no order, just like a little wilderness. I started climbing tiny trees very early, and then bigger trees, and at last big firs and spruces; and I remember in one part of the garden there was a road under the biggest tree, and from there, I could throw cones down on people, and when there was a big ski event, there would be many thousand people coming by. Of course I felt power: I could look down on people. Well, I could at least throw down some things. This feeling of being above and looking, surveying, was very important. Right away came an interest in technology—which branches should be used and which shouldn't be used.

DR: So what you choose out of nature is already technology?

AN: Yes. Already technology, and the way you do it—how far you can reach toward the very top, which gets thinner and thinner—this is technique. How far can one go? This was the beginning of my climbing. The next step was when I went with my only good friend, Halvdan, to his family's hut near Rondane. There was a canyon above a small stream, where we started to explore. Halvdan and I started to climb along the brook . . .

DR: How old were you then?

AN: Thirteen. And the next year was the first time we went up to a big mountain not far away. No technical climbing, but at least

I associated climbing with mountains, and found that tremendously important. Tremendously.

DR: What made it important?

AN: Well, the greatness . . . not only the bigness, but the greatness—the shape, the gestalt of it: It was saying something. This mountain, Smiubæljen (1,916 meters), was a very broad peak with an impression of strength without aggression. Not any kind of aggression. It was so broad and only gradually got narrower toward the summit, with the same benevolent character as Hallingskarvet from a distance. My climbing thus immediately involved a kind of cult of the mountain. We had the idea to get almost to the summit, and beyond there were other mountains rising on and on, and gradually we got this crazy idea to get to the summit of every mountain . . .

DR: So back then it was important to get to the top?

AN: Absolutely.

DR: Not just of one, but of everything?

AN: To get to the top. A little later, when I was twenty or more, the weather was once absolutely idiotic for going to the summit, so I had to crawl on all fours up the last meters, as if that was very important. So there you have quantity again, because we tried to get to the top of as many mountains as possible—counting each mountain, and also calculating the number of kilometers needed for the climb, the distance in kilometers, and then the height. When we went on trips we had a certain way of calculating the amount of climbing. The first mountain on the range went up to, say, 2,000 meters, and the next might only be worth three hundred meters, because we went only a little down and then up again. This was our cult of the mountain. And it was out of the question to take any photographs with us—my good friend and me—in them. It was sacrilegious.

DR: But you did take photographs.

AN: Yes, of the mountains, but not with anybody there.

DR: No people?

AN: Absolutely not. If my friend was in between the mountain and me, he had to go away. It's holy, you see . . . the mountain is holy.

DR: Do you think you captured something of the mountain with these pictures? More because there were no people?

AN: No, that has to do with God. You cannot take a photograph of God.

DR: Right. But even when you decide what to look at, there's a person there, you are putting something in the picture—you, the photographer.

AN: Yes, but that was supposed to be eliminated as much as possible. We tried to experience the mountain as a mountain and not as a person, so to say.

DR: So you should be like a mountain, too?

AN: Yes.

DR: Even when you were first starting, you had this idea?

AN: That first summit had all those talents or attributes I wished to have. And these others, to some extent, also. Not the very sharp and thin ones. They should be heavyset, with more greatness than bigness, solid and in place.

DR: Well, Hallingskarvet looks like a loaf of bread, right?

AN: Yes, to you. I see it more as a great blue whale, rising out of the plateau.

DR: It's a special shape of mountains that's very Norwegian.

AN: Yes. I would say so. The shape of a mountain has much to do with its character.

DR: Do you think you sensed that when you were five, when you were first here?

AN: I don't know. I believe I knew that the mountain didn't

really belong to the earth, that it was something that was touching the heavens.

DR: The ones that pointed up toward the sky were not touching as much as this.

AN: No. That's right. It was kind of a substitute for a good father.

DR: That's probably what you learned later in analysis—a mountain is a substitute for a father. That seems to be humanizing it in a way that you might not originally have wanted.

AN: Yes. But it *was* a kind of protector. It showed me what was worthwhile, suggesting that one should try to be calm and self-contained . . .

DR: . . . and with no people in the picture.

AN: Yes. Impossible.

DR: Did you immediately start doing technical climbing?

AN: When we were thirteen, we started at least doing things that were difficult. I remember a small brook, with cliffs not more than five meters high. But then, when I was fifteen, I started real climbing, in the big mountains. We had a fire escape rope ten meters long, absolutely inelastic—that was the equipment—and then heavy boots, and we went straight to the first real climbing mountain in the highest mountain range in Norway, and we met people who had a tourist hut not far away—marvelous people who were extremely kind to us. My good friend and I were very interested in what we were doing, so we had great respect and fondness for mountain people who were living there, who never would think of climbing themselves, of course.

DR: Why not?

AN: No, it was not a part of the culture of the Norwegian mountain people. When hunting, they would have to climb sometimes, but they understood that we were crazy about it, and in order to see the mountain all the time, I made myself a tent with small holes so that when I was falling asleep, I could still see the mountain, but the holes couldn't be shut, so I was freezing terribly.

DR: Tiny little holes?

AN: Yes, two or three inches square—that was the first of a series of extremely stupid things. It was a terrible life . . . Later, mountaineering became completely established. Mountaineering is a better word than climbing, because it was the mountain itself that interested us, although going to the top was our cult of the mountain. And when we were sixteen and seventeen, I climbed the 106 highest mountains in Norway, and my friend got sick with pleurisy, and after the second year, he was already in the sanatorium. He died ten years later.

DR: Halvdan was your only close friend?

AN: Yes, very close.

DR: So how did his illness affect you?

AN: It should have affected me much more than it did, really. It affected me strongly, but not an overwhelming amount. There, you have this distance again. I didn't visit him in his sanatorium, only 150 kilometers from Oslo. I didn't dare visit him.

DR: Not even one time?

AN: No. But I saw him when he was on vacation from the sanatorium. He went into business before he died. I was really tremendously fond of him, but nevertheless didn't really do enough for him, and that, I think, is typical of me. I thought of him very much, but did not do much.

DR: Thinking and not doing?

AN: Yes.

DR: How did the climbing, you think, connect to the things you were beginning to study and read about in high school?

AN: Well, the philosophers I read had little patience for climbing, except for the mystics, who were after a oneness with nature. But my oneness was such that I was in a kind of contrast with the mountain, because the mountain had all these attributes which I didn't have.

DR: Such as . . . constancy?

AN: Constancy. Equal-mindedness. The mountain had everything in itself, without boasting or arrogance. Sending avalanches and stones only when it had to do it; saying implicitly, "If you care for me, you will never be hit by the stone, because you will study and understand where not to go and when there will be a storm." I continued all my life to think that one is only in danger because of lack of love of the mountain. If you really love the mountain, you will have contact with the whole. There will be storms, but you will survive.

DR: You don't think there is any luck involved? You think people who die in the mountains just don't know enough about them?

AN: There may be a lot of luck, but there is an extremely small chance of anything happening to you if you pay attention.

DR: There are others who might go up into the mountains and look at them and say, "This is an extreme place. It's rough, it's exciting, it's changing all the time, it's sharp, it's the ultimate, it's anything but calm." But you found constancy there.

AN: Yes. But never the same. It never looks the same in the mountains.

DR: Perhaps people find what they want to find.

AN: Yes. What they need. I needed a tough place.

DR: But a calm and tough place.

AN: And a tough place where there is no conflict, so-called dangers but no disputes, whereas with other human beings, there is always some disharmony.

DR: It was an escape from people?

AN: Yes. I think I escaped from people very often.

DR: Have you ever made it back to be comfortable with people?

AN: Yes. But less than one would expect from me. I need distance when we are in nature, for instance . . . not much need for intimacy in the wilds.

DR: Even intimacy between each person and the world outside?

AN: Oh, yes, intimacy with nature. But what we call intimacy between people may be spoiled by words.

Friendship remained cool for me, strangely cool. But the rules of friendship are very, very important, and I was very afraid of violating these rules in a way that I feared few other things. They were always more frightening than anything grasped of the mountain.

II: THE MIND AND THE CIRCLE

A *t the turn of the thirties, where would one go to get closer
to the cutting edge of philosophy? After a few trips to the
Paris of Bergson and élan vital, Arne settled on Vienna, the city
of neurosis itself, an intellectual center on the verge of annihila-
tion by the Nazi threat, home of Freud's psychoanalysis, as well
as the site of the latest movement in philosophy, known as logical empiricism (positivism) developed by a group of philosophers
known as the Vienna Circle.*

*Inspired by the stark claim of Ludwig Wittgenstein that "the
world is the totality of facts, not of things," these men (and a
few women) tried to steer philosophy toward a scrutiny of the
rigors of ordinary speech, aiming to dispense with muddy concepts like truth, the meaning of life, and the metaphysical categories that make possible our everyday experience of reality: basic
ideas like unity, nothingness, change, rest, quantity, and
quality—all general organizing notions that allow us to make any
sense of what happens. What logical empiricism tried to do was
to treat these problems as difficulties of speech, simply the result
of our inability to make our terms clear to one another.*

*Why do it this way? Trying to sketch out the mistier criteria
of thought had led to only more fog: weighty, overgrown systems
of thought that were too complicated and strange to be understood by any but their creators, the systematic philosophers.
Besides, the grand metaphysics of Spinoza and Hegel are so
incompatible with the movement of modern science. The appar-*

ent lack of progress of philosophical questioning led the discipline to flounder in times of social and technological upheaval. So the analytical branch of philosophers in Vienna pulled in their sails and tried to contemplate the most immediate things in syntax and semantics.

The result was that the less-soluble problems began to fade into obscurity. The claim that human conception of the world might be more than the recording of sense impulses is rejected as spurious and mystical, founded on absurd belief. In their push to ascribe certainty to only the most empirical of sensations, the positivists could accept little more than the immediate recognition of sense-data as valid information. It would be inadmissible, for example, to look up in the air and announce, "The sky is blue." That is already a hypothesis. All that we could be completely sure of might be described, albeit somewhat poetically, as: "Blue . . . here . . . now." Anything more would be conjecture. Philosophy forgets about its previously grandiose claims, and instead tries to reinvigorate the language, not with the rich expression of poetry, but with the exaltation of logic as a part of common sense.

This dream of clarity enchanted young Arne Naess. Here was a circle of thinkers who welcomed his eager tough-mindedness, who were ready to take the energetic Norwegian student seriously. They would not follow his mother's lead in chiding him for lack of emotion. He was welcomed into their group, but still the feeling of distance remained, and he was never quite willing to pledge his own allegiance to their view or approach.

Meanwhile, Vienna was also the center for a more concrete kind of personal questioning. By the thirties, Freud's teachings had spawned an entire new field of medicine, dedicated to reaching the workings of the mind and its inner troubles through conversation and interview (not so different from the process Arne and I are engaged in here). Psychoanalysis was still in its infancy when Naess began to undergo serious "treatment," with regular sessions six times a week. In those days, a rigorous program of so many hours on the couch was all that was needed to qualify one as a professional analyst, prepared at the completion to advise and heal patients. Is this what Arne had in mind when he began his course on the couch of Dr. Eduard Hitschman, a disci-

ple of Freud's? Arne denies it. He never intended to practice as a doctor, but only to uncover the past, to find a reason for the distance, the life inside the shell—back to infancy, home to all Freudian neuroses. Here was a different domain for the study of the mind, personalized, if perhaps imprecise. These two activities—philosophical analysis and analysis of the unconscious—occupied Arne's time inside the walls of Vienna, a nervous city at the brink of its own final despair.

Could We Agree to a Formulation Like This?

DR: You went to Austria because it seemed to have enough mountains. And, yet, you found yourself right away a member of the Vienna Circle, the most influential group of philosophers in the early part of this century. How did this happen?

AN: I found even when I was twenty-one that I could go any-where in any university, straight into any kind of room. By chance and luck, I went straight into the graduate seminar of the logical positivists with Moritz Schlick, Rudolf Carnap, Friedrich Waismann, Herbert Feigl, and others. They all worked under the shadow of Ludwig Wittgenstein.

DR: So you felt charmed and accepted wherever you went?

AN: They understood somehow that this boy was very serious—"He is one of us." They were so nice to me as a very young man. It was a miracle that I could be there. Their discussion was tough, but clear, without nonsense.

DR: Did it seem to have the answers for you?

AN: No, not many answers, but clear collaboration of a kind that I could stand. There was a coolness between them in a sense, but tremendous discussions. One phrase at a time, and when somebody disagreed, they did so with caution: "Maybe this isn't adequate . . . Could we agree to a formulation like this?"

DR: So there was a certain aesthetic involved?

AN: A sense of decorum. One never in any way indicated any

enjoyment of disagreement. "If there is disagreement we should see if it is real disagreement or just a difference in manner of speaking." We invited the opponent to join us—"Maybe we could say this. Would you agree to that?" So we really were seeking concord in philosophy, not by emotional appeal, but by trying out different formulations in a completely relaxed way, instead of saying, "I disagree!" Then we could determine if there was a real disagreement or just a dispute over phrasing. It was quite demanding, because real lucidity was needed.

But it was also a special philosophy of language that I didn't like, because I didn't enjoy language. . . . When there was dissent, they might say something like, "Language is constructed in such a way that it is not foreseen that we could say that." So it would be something with language that was not in order, something in the logic of language that was amiss.

DR: Is that the clearest message you could say you got from these people? That something about language needed to be changed?

AN: No, no. If you didn't like a philosophical opinion, somehow you found out that it was against the language.

DR: Against the language, the ordinary language?

AN: Yes.

DR: And this appealed to you?

AN: No, it did not. I enjoyed the artistic way of discussion, which was beneficial for me as a foreigner. There were certain others who were crushed by it, who didn't really belong there.

DR: It seems there was a certain artistry you were after.

AN: Yes, artistry.

DR: It's a little surprising, because you seem to shy away from emotions and the use of language to say beautiful things, and yet something in this method of discussion did touch you.

AN: It was beautiful argumentation!

DR: So argumentation can be beautiful, as music can be beautiful?

AN: Yes. Crisp argumentation, where every word is carefully used.

DR: Like the elegance of a way of climbing up the rock face . . .

AN: . . . and you could always say, "Well, what do you mean by so and so?" And they would answer, "Well, there is still a kind of fogginess here." So this crystal clarity, this hardness as glass, was vital. Carnap was very good, and the others were also good. And they accepted me.

DR: They wanted you to be one of them?

AN: Yes, absolutely. But they were so clever and so fast, so good in language, and I was a foreigner, so I had to think very thoroughly before I said anything. Of course, I was young and eager, so sometimes I used a very interesting kind of trick. I sometimes said, "On the contrary . . ." and then they would stop for a moment and I could say something. What I would say was never stupid. It wasn't very clever, but it was never dumb, so I had a kind of status, because I wouldn't talk without knowing exactly what I wanted to say. They respected that, even if I said, "William James, I think, is nearer the truth than Bertrand Russell." Gasp! That would be terrible!

DR: So you found a place in this group. How many people were there?

AN: About fifteen people. But I would not say I "fit in." They believed in things I didn't believe in. They believed that most philosophical problems were pseudoproblems that could be analyzed and solved by examining inconsistencies in language. And that I absolutely refused because I was interested in nature, and I didn't think that any of the original problems from Thales had been solved. Rarely did you have a question formulated such that every possible interpretation of that formulation gave only pseudoquestions.

DR: So they were giving up a lot of philosophy?

AN: Yes. They went too fast through the job of interpretation, of hermeneutics. When they criticized Martin Heidegger, they pointed out grammatical impossibilities—as if that had much weight in philosophy! It all went back to the point that I was never really enthusiastic about Wittgenstein, whereas they were. And that bothered me. Suddenly, Schlick might ask, "What would Wittgenstein say to this?" And that annoyed me. At first, nobody would respond and then somebody would say, very carefully, "Maybe he would want so-and-so." Ultimately, they, in a sense, never left the position of Frege and Russell, developed by Wittgenstein.

DR: If they were so enamored of Wittgenstein, why didn't they follow the language he did, and write in his very strange, aphoristic way? Because if it's all about language . . .

AN: No, they didn't especially like the way he wrote. It was the content itself: "to get rid of the philosophical muddle."

DR: They couldn't see that the style was tied in with the content? Wittgenstein couldn't have written another way.

AN: No, they didn't see that, and Carnap especially was very much against it. He would say Wittgenstein was a genius, unique and unpredictable. Once, I said just for fun, "I feel that maybe I am underquoted, perhaps in comparison to Wittgenstein." Then he smiled and said, "You think it would be reasonable if we quoted you a little more?" Carnap was cool, like I wanted people to be. In 1940, he felt instinctively that the logical empiricists would take seriously my pragmatic view of language. My view reminded him of the following story:

There was a postman who had to go through the mountains to deliver letters, but he died with his post horn in his mouth. He had a horn to let people know, "Here I am," you know—and he was found because in the springtime they heard a horn. That was the post horn. It made this nice sound when the ice was melting. But the man was dead—the horn should have been heard the season before. I was like that: Whatever I was saying against them, I should have said the year before. By 1940, I agreed. There was no longer any need to argue against them.

Language Unruly and Wild

DR: How would you summarize how their view of language differed from yours?

AN: First of all, I thought that language has no definite system of rules and that if you make a rule saying, This applies to the language, then it is a kind of hypothesis. And if it applies to a definite word, one has to study, say, one hundred occurrences of that word in the text and one hundred occurrences that you take from oral discussions or talks between people. And then, one might say that, given these two hundred occurrences of the use of the word, we may surmise that this hypothesis is likely. Some of them would be overly complicated and would be pushed out immediately, and the same holds true if you make a hypothesis about an ordinary use of a certain term or sentence. Some of them are too complicated to be of use for you, but the ordinary language may be tremendously complicated. But Carnap didn't take such things seriously. He did not believe in what I call "semantics."

DR: It seems that you were advocating some kind of skeptical use of statistics to find out the truth about our use of words.

AN: Not the truth, but a very good hypothesis about how certain terms are used, rules that we as users of ordinary language don't know anything about, even though we use the words all day long. They thought they knew the rules without wanting to test their hypotheses to see if they were accurate.

DR: But it seems that you're taking the logical step from those who want to look into ordinary language for the answers concerning how to talk about things. You're saying, "Let's go ask people with no pretensions to be philosophers." In your monograph, *"Truth" as Conceived by Those Who Are Not Professional Philosophers*, you interviewed "the man and woman on the street" to see what they thought truth was. And this kind of empirical research troubled some of these supposedly empirically minded thinkers, no?

AN: But that was only meant as one percent of an investigation about the problem of truth, because at certain moments I could be extremely skeptical and have this notion that if you had found out enough about empiricism, about how it was put to use, nothing much was left. I gave up this more fanatical empiricism very quickly.

DR: This "fanatical empiricism" was something you learned in Vienna, perhaps?

AN: I am not sure about that. They were not fanatical empiricists. No, they were logical. They believed in a logical grammar of language.

DR: But, at the same time they believed in empirical science.

AN: Yes, but no problem in philosophy is wholly empirical. They imagined they had perfect knowledge of ordinary language about their mother tongue. So, to me, they were antiempirical, as they thought that their analysis of the use of "or," for example, was much deeper than what you could get from statistics.

DR: But nobody had tried statistics in philosophy before, had they?

AN: No. Their whole atmosphere was intuitionist, and I didn't find that especially empirical. They criticized psychologists for accepting things on meager empirical evidence. But they were on something of the right track. Among them, I was considered very intelligent, whereas I didn't see myself as very intelligent, just very independent.

DR: Why did they think you were so intelligent?

AN: Well, I had good counterarguments. And that was very important. I had arguments that were really very difficult to answer.

DR: Did they speak often of politics?

AN: No, surprisingly, but they were close to politics, and they considered their work to be an antifascist, antinationalist undertaking—the unity of science.

DR: So they saw a political side to their work?

AN: Absolutely. But at the meetings I went to, they rarely discussed it. They were active in politics, but at the same time able to maintain a separation from it. They considered dialectical materialism to be just a foggy remnant of bad metaphysics.

DR: So do you think they made an original contribution?

AN: Absolutely.

DR: Even though they didn't leave this position?

AN: Yes.

DR: Where was the originality?

AN: The originality is in the method, because it is so clear.

DR: For your own case, do you think clarity was not so much a virtue?

AN: Yes, an extremely great virtue, but precision is only a tool. How can it help an intuition, such as, "Ultimately, all living beings are one"? Carnap would have been upset by such a statement. And I would say, this is a point of departure that mustn't be lost, because there may be important things that are very difficult to make more precise.

I suppose that the logical empiricists were most interested in preciseness. And, as a consequence, they never became "gurus" for our time, because clarity does not inspire, whereas a man like Heidegger or Wittgenstein can be read forever, because the reader's imagination is intensely engaged. Carnap doesn't let you do that.

DR: Is this an argument for or against precision?

AN: It's for precision, but not for leaving out imprecision. If you leave out the nonprecise things, you are lost in accuracy. One must go back and forth, from precision to ambiguity. Rarely in philosophy can the vague be eliminated. Consider such statements as, "The will is free" or "Ultimately, the universe is spiritual rather than material." Such things should be ignored. But the terminology gets old-fashioned if they are formed in rational language. I think the logical empiricists were very original in pointing this out.

Neurosis and Discovery

DR: Now, did you feel at this time the need to be original yourself? A need, a desire, a want to be original? Is this what led you into psychoanalysis?

AN: I wanted to deepen my own intuitions, my own inclinations and attitudes—to find them out, to criticize some of them. One reason I went into psychoanalysis was to see how my work in philosophy could be improved through more self-knowledge. So I went to an analyst.

DR: Every day?

AN: Yes.

DR: For how long?

AN: Fourteen months, without any stop. I went Monday through Saturday.

DR: Tough to find time for climbing. I'm interested in the connection between philosophy and psychoanalysis here, the link, how you moved over. Was it a struggle between the two, or did it seem like a natural extension? Were other people connecting these two as well?

AN: Well, I thought psychoanalysis would be an indispensable auxiliary discipline to philosophy, just like symbolic logic. You can use symbolic logic and you can use psychoanalysis in order to see that very often you may jump to certain conclusions that are in harmony with unconscious conceptions you might have, for example, from infancy. So I took it pragmatically, as a tool, and I also found Socrates' "Know thyself" to be an imperative to self-analysis. And psychoanalysis teaches you to look in a most brutal way at your emotions and values, with bitter clarity—not brutality, but ferocious honesty.

I was told that Ibsen was really trying to dissolve every kind of dishonesty: Peer Gynt was through and through a dishonest person, and Brand was through and through honest, revealing the limitation of his honesty. With honesty, you get into a kind of destructiveness. Well, never mind. Psychoanalysis was then at the peak of its influence in Europe, and Vienna was the center. So it was impossible to be in Vienna without discussing Freud versus both Adler and Jung.

DR: Were some of these other philosophers you came in contact with also undergoing analysis?

AN: Yes, several others. All my acquaintances.

DR: So it was not something that was thought of as only a cure for disease?

AN: No. It was a cure for some people, but among the authors and the scientists, it was quite popular as an aid to self-discovery. In Vienna, at that time, the state itself was neurotic. It was only a head without a body, lacking Hungary after the empire was dissolved. It was a terribly difficult time, and there was an enormous amount of neurotic people, I think, but gifted, as you know—a time known as Wittgenstein's Vienna.

But my direct connection was through a Norwegian student. He thought that as a fellow Norwegian, I should drink a lot of beer and sit around in restaurants with other Norwegians and have a terrible time, and in the evenings go looking up girls and have a good time, and so on. And when he asked me, I said, "No, I'm going to an organ concert in a church." (There were fabulous organ concerts in fabulous churches, a fantastic experience to be in such big churches with such tremendous organs.) So he heard this, and he thought I was very queer, and he thought, This man needs analysis.

He was in psychoanalysis with Dr. Hitschman. So he told him about this Norwegian who seemed to be schizophrenic, but not beyond being saved. He didn't tell me about that, but he said, "There is an analyst, Dr. Hitschman, who is also interested in Norwegian literature, especially Knut Hamsun, and he might take you if you are interested." I said, "Yes, I am certainly interested in analysis." So I went to Hitschman and he accepted me immediately. He had only seven patients, because he liked to have them come every day, so he said I could come every day at eight o'clock in the morning.

DR: Was this a big expense for you?

AN: Yes, it was a tremendous expense. I had to use nearly all my money for it. So we started and after a week he said, "Well, I can tell you, Naess, you are not schizophrenic." And I said, "Huh?" He replied, "Your friend told me that you might be schizophrenic." It was very difficult because of my specialty: philosophy. He would say, "Tell me exactly what's going on in your mind." And then I tried to describe the contents of my consciousness.

. . . Suddenly, I would see a little thing in the corner of the window or something and in order to describe what I saw, it would take many minutes, and during those minutes I would have a stream of consciousness of tremendous complexity. I suppose it is to Hitschman's credit that after a week he didn't consider me a schizophrenic. First of all, I saw that I should talk about things that were more painful for me to talk about or private like sexuality or really naughty things I had done. But this analysis proceeded, and after some weeks it was clear that I had a real serious infantile neurosis and that my behavior and my thinking were still expressions of that neurosis, even if somewhat adapted to society. So it didn't hurt me; I was not a patient.

DR: But you should still come for fourteen months?

AN: There were a lot of things that could be obstacles. He was, for instance, intrigued that I was talking so much about girls and having nothing to do with them.

DR: You were having nothing to do with girls?

AN: No, not seriously, not sexually. So he thought it was probably not a good thing to be like that. I was a miser with my time, and he hadn't seen anybody who was so miserly with his time. These were things that I understood to be obstacles for development. He was a very fat and big old man, probably over sixty years old, and he didn't understand this climbing business at all. It was clear that he didn't like what I was doing there.

DR: Part of the neurosis?

AN: He thought it was part of the neurosis. It was a masochistic trend, for instance, when I forgot my ski poles.

DR: And how about the philosophy you were studying?

AN: Oh, he certainly didn't like that very much. I was invited to the home of a very famous man, a professor, and I told Hitschman with relish where I had been. And he then said something insulting about professors. You see, he liked Freud, but he had not a high opinion of academic life. I thought his remark was uncalled for. He then said, "What do you say there? How do you think this is motivated? How does it connect with what you dreamt last night?" I was never supposed to talk to him during the analysis session.

DR: You were just sitting on the couch.

AN: Yes, like this. Then I might say, "It's really very expensive to undergo analysis." And he said, "Well, you know, I can only have very few students or patients, especially when I see them every day." And that was one of the ten times when my esteem for him went down.

DR: It was only a very particular kind of person who could afford to go, someone who had so much time free every day.

AN: Yes. Or where there was a socialist government, some did not have to pay. There was a kind of ethics there. There should be a distance between the patients and the analyst of such a profound kind that the analyst would never reveal any standpoint apart from the analysis of motivations, causes, and consequences: never judging, never explaining his own views or his monetary affairs. Also, I once said, "I saw your daughter and it would be nice to know more, know her more," and I knew that was against the rules.

DR: Yes.

AN: Analysis must be completely direct and immediate. So he started to explain the obvious rule that analysts would try to keep their families away from the patients. Oh, he said it in a very nice way, but you see that on the whole the distance that developed in my infancy was very near to what I felt should be the general relationship between people! They should never judge each other. They should just explore motivations. If someone hit me in the face, that would be astonishing. I would try to find out why it happened. I would not complain at all. "What's going on in you now, why did you hit me?" "This, of course," Hitschman would say, "is a scientific attitude."

DR: You wanted everything to be so scientific?

AN: I wanted to be scientific as much as possible, and in my doctoral thesis, which I was writing at the time, I talked much about observation and used the analogy of somebody coming from another planet, investigating people speaking and people running and people making a lot of noises. And they would then analyze the sentence, "The sun is 150 million kilometers from Earth." They would then hear this noise and see the things they write, and they would reconstruct astronomy without having any recourse to looking at the sky, because they would see the interconnection of what they were writing with the instruments they were using, and so on.

I had this notion that a scientist should look at himself as a complete stranger, and society is a completely strange affair. That was how I constructed a behaviorist epistemology in my doctoral thesis. And, you see, this was possible for me to do, quite consistent with my own distance from other people and from my point of view.

An analyst might say, "This dream here we usually interpret as a sign of homosexuality." Then I would unconsciously or preconsciously talk more about the dream and a relation to what I had done in the last day or something, in order to cooperate. I would not say, "No, no, Doctor. No, no. I never had any—Heh." And that, of course, was a little artificial, because if I were completely spontaneous, I would say, "Ho, ho, oh, no," and then say, "Well, let me see, let me see the dream once more," and start to find out a little more about the circumstances before it—but that would be going against the rule of saying everything going on in my consciousness. Anything having to do with homosexuality at that time, 1934, was far more taboo than it is today.

DR: And especially if you hadn't had much experience with women and someone was telling you this, you probably wouldn't want to hear it.

AN: No, but of course I was sure that there was nothing there. I mean, nothing in the prior relation to the girls was intense. Yes. So this analysis then went on and on, and I simply couldn't stand living like a prisoner in Vienna. I complained to Hitschman. So he said, "Well, then, I'm sure you could get papers that would qualify you to practice psychoanalysis after only two more months."

DR: (Laughs)

AN: "Two months. You could get the full testimony. And you would be a member of the psychoanalytical society, and you could start seeing patients if you wish . . ."

DR: Start on your own?

AN: But I didn't take two more months.

DR: (Laughs) You couldn't . . .

AN: Even if I wasn't sure I wanted to be a teacher, I was certain I wouldn't be an analyst. So I stopped and he of course thought this was a pity, but we were good friends and he wrote many letters to me, although I wrote little to him. He gave me some offprints, which I still have—one that says, "To Arne Naess, who will aim his sights high." He was sorry I never ended up an analyst myself.

The Philosopher at the Clinic

DR: Why? Did he think you'd be good at it?

AN: I don't know. He understood that I was talented in some way and was willing to analyze things in a very cool manner. They probably needed good young people for the future of the movement. So he wanted me to consider psychiatry at the same time, for instance going to a psychiatric clinic and doing some analysis of the patients there, in a tentative way.

DR: He wanted you to analyze them?

AN: No, to make observations and talk to them and find out about them.

DR: As an expert or just as a student?

AN: As a student. He opened every door, saying to the head of the psychiatric clinic, "Dr. Arne Naess is a young, very talented man, and he should be free to come to the clinic and do whatever he finds interesting." So I went there in the evenings, and it was tremendously interesting.

DR: So in the clinic, you walked around dressed as a regular doctor in the white robes and such?

AN: Yes, and it was somewhat ridiculous, because the graduate students and young doctors made the rounds every morning at ten or eleven o'clock, visiting the patients. The chief doctor, Pötzl himself, would then ask a couple of questions, and behind the young doctors came the graduate students, and they went along very solemnly—and suddenly, I would appear in the opposite direction after my own tour of inspections of my own patients, you see?

DR: Did you feel close to your patients?

AN: Yes, it was ridiculous, since I had no standing at all. But I had at least three patients who I really followed intensively, and I developed a new view of the suffering of humankind. I was especially close to one—a woman about twenty-five years old, who seemed at first completely rational and sound. I wondered whether they could have made a mistake putting her in there. I had long talks with her, and she said that soon she would get a terrible relapse, into a paranoic, schizophrenic state; she could foresee this, because already it was the third time that she was picked up out of the Danube for trying to commit suicide because of a relapse into a psychotic state of suffering—and it was in the autumn. The first symptom was that she had an irrational urge to look up a friend of hers, and a certain time after that, she would get sick again.

DR: Each time?

AN: Yes. And now she expected another relapse. One morning I heard screams—there were always screams, but this was more chilling than ever. I saw her in a straitjacket, screaming.

DR: Did you feel at the time that you had any special ability to help her?

AN: Yes, and that's what made me both sensitive to the full range of human suffering and aware of the ocean of possibilities one has for really helping other people. I saw that just sitting there made a difference to her.

DR: Was it anything special in your character or education that trained you to help her, or were you just a sympathetic person?

AN: Yes. Some people said I looked kind. I thought that if they got to know me better they would not take me to be an especially kind person.

DR: Now, how did this connect to the fact that you always felt a distance between yourself and other people?

AN: That's a curious thing, that distance may very well go together with a feeling of sympathy, empathy, and grasp of how much affliction there is all around. I knew of anguish from my infancy. Longing, first of all. The yearning for the impossible as far as I could see, because I didn't recognize it as an object.

It made a tremendous impact on me to sit there with another human being, and once she had a clear enough moment to say, "Now I am completely crazy." It helped her to have somebody in the neighborhood. She was in a small room, alone, in a straitjacket, and there was distress and panic. What a fate: to sit alone like that, for hours and hours every day, and with no prospect except to get out and then try to kill herself.

DR: From your experience with it, did the field of psychiatry offer any cure for this?

AN: At that time, paranoid-schizophrenic people had little hope. So they were sent to a particular institution, where they were simply put away, like old furniture that should not be destroyed but somehow just kept around. They would be sent to Steinhof. Some of them knew of Steinhof and the possibility that they would be sent there, and there was a lot of screaming.

DR: And from there, there was no return?

AN: It was bleak. I hope that this patient I have talked about got out of the clinic and was successful in suicide. From that time, I viewed suicide as a very natural thing that many people could commit for good reasons.

DR: Is that because life itself is not of value, with only a certain kind of life, a certain quality of life, worth living?

AN: *Life is wonderful, delightful, and fantastic, but to be alive is a completely different thing.* Under certain circumstances, it is so awful that suicide should not be discouraged. I am talking about cases where someone has been suffering a long time and it's quite clear that they would prefer to stop living. We are all going to stop, we all have limited time, and it's not of value to go on as long as possible. Reasonable people, after cool reflection, may prefer to stop, to have an abrupt close, and look back to some good memories, and decide it is enough.

I never seriously thought I would be a psychiatrist, but I was grateful to all those who showed me these things. Much later, I gave a lecture to the students of Oslo University on the meaning of life, because so many young people search for something they can do that really would make a difference for humanity. I said, "Well, it's very easy, just sit down. Sit down with somebody who is in extreme pain." It's tremendously simple if you have some empathy. Go out to either the prisons or the clinics. I was not the same person after I heard those screams.

The Promise of Behavior

DR: You used some of your psychoanalytic experience to develop your own kind of behaviorist approach to methodology and epistemology.

AN: I use this distance that you do not speak. You immediately hear the other person's words as symptoms of something. Every sentence reveals motivations. Imagine an anthropologist observing a dance of the Trobriand Islands. The researcher of the dance would not use the classification they would use in New York, but would be completely open for whatever it could mean, this dance. The meaning of the dance cannot be grasped spontaneously, but only over a long period of time, in which its significance as part of behavior is comprehended.

DR: But one tries to appropriate the dance from a whole other culture, you know. You come with some preconceived notions to try and find a way to judge it.

AN: Yes. Then we should have a minimum in common. And our judgment will always be tentative.

DR: How is this behaviorist?

AN: It's behaviorist in the philosophical sense of going immediately for the meaning of the behavior. You find the meaning of the behavior through the next behavior and the succession of the behaviors.

DR: Would you still hold to this view?

AN: No, and it ended there. My doctoral thesis concluded with a behavioral model of research, and there may be many other models of behavior — or models of research. I still take it as a very interesting special viewpoint.

DR: But limiting also?

AN: Oh, yes, of course, but it is, in a sense, complete. It's a complete model of epistemology. But limited, because it is just one of many models. Even in his quantum physics, Niels Bohr also somehow ends up with all this apparatus of forces and equations. You get back again to the laboratory with concrete experiments, and you don't analyze those activities in themselves. And then this fantastic universe with electrons and so on becomes preliminary to the making of atom bombs. You discover that this behavior with such-and-such raw materials might end with a tremendous explosion. (Laughs)

DR: So from here you returned. You left Vienna for good. Disillusioned . . . ?

AN: No, no, not at all.

DR: . . . or ready for the next step?

AN: Yes, and with a suitcase full of pitons, for climbing in the

Alps. I embarked on this—not behaviorist, but behavioral—epistemology. If I was to go on with this, the next thing would be an empirical study of something concrete. So I turned to rats—and California.

III: RATS IN CALIFORNIA

A few years ago, I took a trip to the American desert with Arne Naess. First, we went to the Grand Canyon, but he told me this was too grand. We had to leave, and drive across the state of Arizona, in search of the most perfectly ordinary place we could find. Somewhere not spectacular, but a place we could dwell in and make our home for several days — where we could sit in one place to work in the morning, in another to work in the afternoon, in another to build a fire, and in another to sleep: a home in nature, without walls, but with our presence as part of the land.

Finding this, however, was no small task. We spent the better part of a week meandering around the whole state, looking for a place that was ordinary enough for our purposes. It was difficult to satisfy Arne; every place we stopped seemed too vast and unusual. So we pressed on along highways and dry washes. The exact level of ordinariness proved to be harder to find than the grandest of canyons.

Arne learned his love for the free yet elusive desert on his first trip to California, in 1938. He was invited to Berkeley by the "gurus" of behaviorism to pursue his interest in making philosophy and empirical science something that could be empirically observed in both humans and other animals. Why look at rats? Because they are so ordinary? Because they are like us, or far away from us? Is it a coincidence that their Latin scientific name is Rattus norvegicus? *In the end, who is the subject of the experi-*

ment? Arne moved from watching the behavior of the rats to watching the behavior of the scientists watching the rats. Each could be reduced to its behavior, but each remains something more in the end.

The psychology department at Berkeley was happy at the time to let this curious foreign philosopher loose in their laboratories. Years later, Naess returned to the University of California, this time in the turmoil of 1968. Things had changed. Even the rats were no longer so innocent. And it was harder than ever to find a simple place, far away from expectation.

We are Super Rats

DR: So how did you happen to head for California?

AN: Well, California was always, in my mind, something like an *eventyr*—this word is difficult to translate.

DR: Somewhere in between a fairy tale and an adventure.

AN: Yes. So in 1938, I decided to go there with my wife for the first time, to look at the mountains and the desert. We went there, and it turned out that some people already knew of my thesis on behaviorism. So I entered the university, as usual, like a tempest, storming the gates. I got acquainted with E. C. Tolman, the pioneer in empirical psychology. And I was then eager to make some philosophical experiments with rats.

DR: Why?

AN: I was interested in epistemology, continuing the line from the doctoral thesis, but with less dogma. I would see whether rats could still be decisive when they had many choices. I made a kind of apparatus, where they had to jump longer and longer to get food. And then I had four, eight, and sixteen possible routes. The more possibilities, the more confused they got, and they lost the courage to jump, and would instead try another place and try to jump to the food. They went back and forth, just like people who are not sure where they can best cross a stream. And they were defecating frequently, a sign of disliking a situation.

DR: Just like people?

AN: No. This was . . . (Laughs) And I had three rooms. One office and two rooms for experiments with rats. At the Psychology Institute at the University of California, I had assistants who would do all the work, people to make the apparatus, and so on. I acted like a famous foreign scholar. And after that time, coming back to Norway, my reputation got smaller and smaller. (Laughs) At Berkeley, I was at my peak.

DR: Did you consider this to be philosophy?

AN: Absolutely, because it shed light on human anxiety and the extremely indeterminate way the human brain is made. Because of our brain, we are capable of infinitely many choices.

DR: So you're assuming that humans are a bit like rats here?

AN: Yes, we are super rats. Or at least I thought so then; I always saw more possibilities than my friends who were either left or right. I felt I could never take a proper stand, as there was this terrible difficulty in seeing so many possibilities. Action is, in a sense, absolute and dogmatic. You do one thing, and millions of possibilities at that moment are just neglected. How can you really do one thing forcefully when at the same time you see the other possibilities?

DR: So you were studying rats to find out about yourself?

AN: Yes, I was studying rats because they were easier to experiment with. It would be much simpler to see the connection between how far they would be able to jump when they had only one choice, compared to when they had sixteen.

DR: Now, why did you assume people were like rats?

AN: Well, I didn't assume that we were like or unlike them, but there is one particular aspect of life that's shared by every living being who has a certain capacity and nervous development: to see different possibilities and choose among them. So I saw this as a general problem of living beings.

Too Many Possibilities . . .

DR: So was the conclusion something like: People should accept all the possibilities they have and not try and shut out the extra options as they choose just one?

AN: If there is inescapable decrease of forcefulness in action with seeing many possibilities, it started after the evolutionary development of the rats! But my conclusions were never statistically significant. I think that for human beings, it would be significant if I had found a good reason to limit one's perspective in critical situations in life. I think that some people see so many possibilities that they are, for example, unable to marry. In wartime, you have to make certain abrupt choices and stick to them. If you are in a very big forest and you always get distracted by many tiny paths, it is easy to get lost. If you are too aware of these other possibilities, you might die, because you never walk far enough away from where you are. Only then will you reach the border of the forest.

I see many young people who are very bothered by alternatives. They are good at singing, good at football, good at poetry, and they don't know where to go. So I think the problem is real and it has philosophical ramifications, and for me it was tremendously important at that time to state that every problem has an empirical component. I thought it was, so to say, my duty to take the empirical component seriously, because, at that time, I wished to be an empiricist of some kind the rest of my life.

DR: Oh, yes?

AN: I only gave that up in 1968.

The Desert

AN: In Berkeley in the springtime of 1939, I also discovered the desert, which was completely overwhelming in its beauty. The stark, rough rock, the best white sand—this contrasted with the fabulous richness and variety of life in the springtime that pops up through this mineral world, to form millions and millions of tiny flowers. And you had many more animals at that time in the Mojave, tortoise and lizards galore, and very few people! We could buy a hundred-dollar car, drive into the desert along the streams, and have all the landscape for ourselves. We could camp in the vertical rocks, with three-story camps, each story on a different rock ledge: one ledge with a dining room on it, another for the bedroom, and then the toilet—mostly very exposed and difficult to climb to. In this climate, we had to keep still during the middle of the day, but in the evening and the morning it was perfect for exploring. During the night itself, we were just in sleeping bags without a tent, and we looked up at the stars and slept with the stars moving slowly around the heavens. In the morning before sunrise, we started with a cup of tea over a fire burning a small piece of cacti. It was totally different from outdoor life in Norway.

DR: Did you find it easier to think out there?

AN: Yes, but there were also many distractions, because of all the animals, the colors—everything was exciting in the desert. From that time on, the long, cold, rainy periods of the North were a little more difficult to stand without longing for the desert. The wild sands of America competed with the Norwegian mountains for my attention.

Climbing out there was so nice. Climbing every day on small cliffs and small peaks was a much more wholesome, many-sided activity than climbing big mountains, where you could do nothing except climb. So this discovery of the desert, together with the rats, made this Berkeley stay in 1938-39 a coming of age for myself as a sovereign person with a discovery of the rest of the world.

I seek the meaningful wherever I go. But it gets too strenuous if I find maximum meaningfulness all the time. I have an institute of petrology, of chemistry, of hydrology, of zoology, of botany, in my hut or out in the desert—for fun, to some extent, but my activities in these areas reveal my abnormal respect for science.

DR: Yet you didn't find that scientists, by and large, loved the world in the way you did?

AN: No, to my great astonishment.

DR: Do you think that many philosophers love the world?

AN: Not very many. They don't love what they are investigating.

But some philosophers, of course, like Leibniz, pretend this is a perfect place.

DR: Best of all possible worlds, yes?

AN: The most perfect world there could be! And then others say, "My God, is it really that . . . ?"

Psychologists in the Zoo

DR: Now, somewhere along the line, you moved to the idea of studying the scientists who study rats.

AN: Of course, that was a continuation of the doctoral thesis. I found that I was becoming the kind of philosopher who circles roughly around the problem at a very imprecise level, not really doing the job properly. My doctoral thesis was exactly an example of what I was criticizing the philosophers for: circling around the tenets of behaviorism without conducting any real empirical research, which I so respected. So it was my duty to do experiments along the lines of behavioral epistemology with people.

In Berkeley, I had some of my colleagues, psychologists, observing rats, and I sat behind them, observing their behavior while they were watching the rats. And I noted everything—for instance, an airplane passing over the building. This kind of thing was not included in their data. Their practice wouldn't include reporting that, so I reported it, and by observing the movement of the head of the psychologist, I could conclude that he was then writing about what he observed. I traced the curve, which had to do with the behavior of the rats, by observing the psychologist's head.

DR: So what do you think this project taught you? What did it show?

AN: It showed that my idea would take a lot of work, and I soon gave it up. While in Berkeley, I met Karl Popper, and I talked about this. He was aghast and said, "This is a kind of zoology you are doing," and I said, "Yes, sure. That is exactly what I am doing. It is zoology." (Laughs) "But you say you do logical research and you are . . ."

DR: . . . making up the rules. You were cheating?

AN: Cheating, yes. You talk about how you conduct purely empirical research, but you are really using a lot of psychological and other premises. And that's what they were saying in logical empiricism, so I was taking them more seriously than they did themselves.

DR: Yes, they had their own premises. Everyone has their logical assumptions, however empirical they claim to be.

AN: Well, they claimed to be doing logical research and logical science. And they had absolutely a lot of empirical assumptions. On the other hand, as logical empiricists, they had, of course, logical assumptions. But that latter point was not my special point. My special point was pure observation and the importance of observation.

DR: What were some of the assumptions that you didn't realize you had?

AN: I never realized I had very specialized assumptions. Doing experiments, you require a lot of assumptions.

DR: Right. What kind?

AN: For instance, the notion that the rats need food, the idea that they run around the maze just to find the food as soon as possible, because they only get food once a day. That is an assumption, and it is to some extent wrong, because even if they haven't had much food, they have an urge for investigation, which is at least as strong as in humans, a sense of curiosity. Some rats took a long time before they knew the way as well as the others—not because they were slow learners, but because their urge to explore was less pronounced. As you know, they are just as good as humans when learning certain kinds of mazes. Just as good as us.

DR: Yes, I remember doing some of these experiments with mazes when I was about twelve or thirteen years old. But the most I remember of it now was just trying to keep the rats from escaping, how they would often get hurt, climbing out of the maze, which had a glass cover.

AN: So you, too, had a craze for rats?

DR: Yes, it was an experiment I did at school.

AN: At school! We never had such things in Norway.

DR: I don't remember what conclusions came out of it. It was a special program for kids like me who got bored in regular classes. But the whole program was certainly descended from the very work you and your colleagues pioneered in Berkeley. . . .

AN: Oh. But you see, when I came back to Oslo and was suddenly made a full professor, one of the first things I did was to make funds available for continuing some of these rat experiments, which I never really finished. And my colleagues were aghast that the new professor of philosophy was building mazes for rats. I said to Professor Winsnes, "I have learned as much from my rats as I have learned from Plato." And he didn't answer.

It Is True If It Is So

DR: Well, they were already sort of angry at you for doing this other work on "nonprofessional truth." Weren't there some professors who threatened to resign if you turned in this *"Truth" as Conceived by Those Who Are Not Professional Philosophers*?

AN: Yes, there was my adviser, Professor Anathon Aall, who said, "You should absolutely compete, because if you are declared competent, this will make you able to do something." He was the one who said to me, confidentially, "I have read your book on *'Truth' as Conceived* . . . , and if you send in that with other publications, I will not be able to place you as number one." And that, of course, was one of the reasons I had to send it in. I couldn't stop it. My opinion was that it was a very original work, well worth attention.

DR: What was it he objected to?

AN: I think he thought it was undignified.

DR: Because it was too statistical? Too psychological?

AN: I used questionnaires. At that time, 1937-38, they were looked upon as the absolute bottom of doing research. They couldn't be taken seriously at all. And then it implied that I had an undignified, really atrocious view of one of the great problems of humanity—namely, the problem of truth. Taking seriously what these schoolboys and housewives were saying was a kind of caricature of philosophy.

DR: And how did you defend your work against this criticism?

AN: I thought it was very easy to defend it. One component of what we mean by truth is empirical and has to do with the uses of the term in everyday life. And we have only very limited knowledge about how we use the term ourselves. So the hypotheses of people who are not philosophers may be on par with some of the hypotheses of philosophers. They are extremely different, with very important differences. You can find the pragmatists, you can find the different kinds of empiricists . . .

DR: Different from each other, but were their views different from views of the philosophers?

AN: Potentially, some of them were, but mostly they were within the traditions of philosophy. I would say I think there are about thirteen interesting differences in the use of the terms "true" and "false." And one of the uses I found was the one that Alfred Tarski says is the right one—with no kind of justification at all. And that is "-p: it rains." It rains, with a hyphen like this, is true if and only if it rains. And ordinary people would say that a sentence is true if it is the case. An even nicer answer to the question, "What's the common characteristic of every sentence that is true?" is, That *it is so*. There are many others; for instance, that it is shown. That's the verification theory of truth, which has very big weaknesses, of course. And then you have an answer something like, It works—the pragmatist view.

DR: So would you say that this shows that philosophers do speak for the range of opinions in the majority of the population?

AN: Yes. I think that the study of what ordinary people think doesn't make you aware of many new possibilities, but it makes you aware of different uses and functions of the terms "true" and "false." And it makes you aware that what the philosophers say may not be based on tremendous work so much as it is a strange blend of the accepted and the unusual. They use expressions from everyday life, and then they take the examples from Einstein's relativity theory, whereas ordinary people also take their examples from their own experiences. I dislike the philosophers' pretentious kinds of examples and their arrogance toward what I call the commonsense view.

DR: So you're in agreement with those philosophers who want to go back to common sense?

AN: Yes, to make real empirical studies of the use of terms, and then take that as one component of the study—only one component, though.

DR: Is common sense something you make an empirical study of, or do you just say, That's common sense? Is it obvious?

AN: Well, the term "common sense" is, of course, very limited, but how people talk is important—how people actually talk, and philosophers know very little about that. We make errors all the time on the way terms are used, and that makes for many misunderstandings.

Not Enough Like Rodents

DR: So do you recommend that philosophers should do careful experimental work, or should they just pay more attention to ordinary people?

AN: I would like essentially much more cooperation. Some should do really good hard work in statistics—like now in ecology, where Lester Milbrath collects important data about people's opinions on environmental problems in different countries. Terms like "true" and "false" have so many meanings. We need much more awareness of the differences, when you are doing conceptual analysis and logical research. I thought it was nice to see the richness and diversity. And I still think that. But at that time, it was a kind of fanaticism. I went too far.

DR: Oh?

AN: Certainly. I went too far.

DR: Why? Why did you go too far?

AN: Because I was not an integrated person. When I see one path, I stick to that path much too closely, in a sense.

DR: You weren't enough like a rat?

AN: No, especially in music. Instead of grasping the structure of the whole, I was obsessed with one piece at a time, only one. For instance, Schumann's A minor piano concerto. There is this cadenza. [He hums the beginning.] I worked on that for months—work in the sense of learning all the many possibilities open for the pianist. An artist would never get so lost in alternatives . . .

DR: Well, many artists are obsessed by single themes, single ideas.

AN: You think so?

DR: Oh, sure. Lots of them do the same thing over and over again.

AN: And other people get less and less out of it.

DR: Well, it depends.

AN: Well, if you are Bach, of course you can go on in the same vein forever.

DR: Stravinsky said that he put many constraints on himself so that the expression would be deeper in the end. But it doesn't often sound like that when you listen to the music. It doesn't sound especially constrained.

AN: But in Bach, one has the feeling of constraint, though there is complete richness at the same time.

DR: On the other hand, when you study the music of Bach, you always learn how it bends the rules. If you try to analyze it as just a series of rules, the music is lost, and it is the music, not the analysis, that survives through generations.

AN: Sure. That's also said about great performing artists some-times. They just leave the manuscript for a moment and come back again.

DR: So you were in Berkeley when you heard that you had been named professor back home—the University of Oslo's only full professor of philosophy—at the age of twenty-seven?

AN: Yes. I showed the letter to my colleagues. And they said, "Oh, this is unfortunate, tremendously unfortunate, Arne." But Egon Brunswik, my closest friend in the psychology department, said, "Well, even this will not ruin Naess." I would be just as crazy as before.

Bitten by Wild Animals

DR: You returned to Berkeley many times over the years, and recently have spent several terms teaching at Santa Cruz. But the time I remember you being most affected was a visit during the infamous spring of 1968.

AN: Yes, it was, of course, completely fantastic. I liked it very much. I remember I was lecturing on Heidegger in an extremely serious way. I told the students, "You all have to have *Being and Time*" and it was only available in hardcover.

DR: It is still only in hardcover.

AN: And the students just sabotaged my plan; they didn't buy it. They were looking for some existentialist kind of sermons, you see. One of my teaching assistants said, "At least half of them are high." I said, "You mean tall?" "No, they are high!" And a lot of them were certainly on marijuana, at least. The teaching assis-tant said we could see in their essays which ones were stoned, because they may be good essays but suddenly the subject would change or the writing might suddenly become impossible to read. I was very curious, and I remember a certain gifted student said to me, "Everyone over thirty years old is a coward. You won't take any drugs. You professors are so square." That provoked me to say, "I can take anything, because I am so old and arthritic that nothing can happen to me," and then she invited me for a session with LSD, and she acted like a mother and was extremely nice. "You should first take marijuana and then LSD for certain complicated reasons," she said. And we did. I had a marvelous experience but *not* overwhelming, and I said, "It's not overwhelming." She was provoked, and at a new session, she ordered a really fantastic dose of LSD, and there was a marvelous experience of paintings, the room and everything . . . First of all, the room was curved and strange, and my own body seemed to be miles long. Suddenly, I saw some of these paintings of Picasso. For the first time in my life, they made a real impact on me. I was also myself somehow painting a Picasso. That was fabulous. Then my guru—she was then a guru—said, "Maybe we should listen to music." When I was about to say yes, I said to myself, "Why should I say yes? It's been such a long time since she said anything." So, you have this time dilation, which is also interesting philosophically. But then listening to one of the favorites from the time of Bach, something Baroque, I got a very pleasant and good feeling from the music, but not very different from the usual. Later I thought, "There's a difference—you can, from this narcotic, deeply feel things in areas you haven't felt before, but where you have gone there deeply before, it wouldn't help you." It wouldn't help me in music, I thought, but it would help me to understand art.

DR: So what do you think you learned philosophically from this?

AN: Well, again it was a confirmation of a kind of possibilist view. There are universes that are with certain chemicals and then there are other universes that are with chemicals of different kinds. But then I must relate that there was a big crisis in the evening, because the telephone rang. My guru pointed at the telephone and said, "Careful, reality there. It's reality." It was my last day in Berkeley and I thought it might be something having to do with an examination or with my job, and if I didn't answer the telephone, they would come. Very few knew my telephone number, so I said I must take the phone; I didn't understand how I could move to the telephone, but that seemed to be completely easy. So I grabbed the telephone and I listened, and there was talk about somebody being bitten by a wild animal in South America, and it was an old woman's voice. And I said, "I am in the United States. I am not bitten. Somebody else is bitten." I was confused. And then, suddenly, I was clear and I understood it was a student who had not delivered his final essay because he had been bitten and was in the hospital. This was his mother, and she asked me if he could send it later or something, and I said, "Yes!" with unnecessary joy. She probably couldn't understand why I was so delighted! That was OK, but this portion of LSD was so very powerful that I felt later in the night that there was no way at all I could get out of this house and make it to the airport.

DR: This was the last night of your stay?

AN: Yes. So at three o'clock in the morning, I called up one of the real delightful students I had, saying, "I am completely stoned and I don't know how I can clean up the stove. Can you come at seven o'clock in the morning?" "Yes, yes!" he said, and he came and arranged the house and took me to the airport. And there was something strange: some kind of film on the plane about the Soviets putting LSD into the water supply. I have never met anyone else who has heard of such a movie . . .

DR: Didn't you bring some LSD back to Norway?

AN: Yes. I took it up here to Tvergastein. It was impossible for the students to see me go back to Norway without a little LSD. So I had a session with Jon Wetlesen in the wintertime, going naked around the cottage, which was a delightful thing, on LSD. But I remember I was going to cut some wood with an ax, and he said, "No, Arne, you shouldn't use an ax, please don't use an ax!"

But that was an innocent time, when all the bright students used such things, and they stopped using it when, for instance, they tried to get a job. They would immediately cut their hair and be completely straight for a little while. But when weak students with problems, psychological or otherwise, started, everything went wrong. They got hooked and there were tragedies upon tragedies. But in '68 it was still a thing of innocence and strong persons could get away with it. Now, of course, we are more cognizant of the dangers.

DR: And yet you have always been ready to take chances, in order to grasp the full range of possibilities life offers?

AN: Yes, in the early fifties, I was eagerly reading Kierkegaard and later had the impression that there was something tremendously important in his dimension of depth in human beings, that they can't admit they have a life that will soon end. This makes it important how they live. And how they live can only be taken up as a problem if you go to the very bottom of your self, asking, What do you wish with your life? And if you then have a kind of answer, at any definite moment, you must be aware of whether this is in harmony with your overall goals. This makes for what Kierkegaard calls "inwardness," because in inwardness you can keep a kind of consciousness that you know you are living and that this moment is important. And such a thought immediately elicits the question of whether you need some kind of articulated system—a total view—so that you can see, given a situation, whether you are acting in accordance with the deepest intuition of what's worth doing in life.

But whatever system you make looks backward, it's a reflection on the past, and now we have a new situation. So, you must always adapt the conclusion that you will not follow the past—the future is something completely different and, therefore, say it in a very simple way: If the system says to go to the left, one should breathe deeply three times and then say, "I am going to the right! To hell with everything I have thought before!" It is impossible to have it all, so we look at the system and try to find out which would be the minimum change in order to make it decent and justified to go to the right instead of to the left. We might need to change the system, because of observation or some new data—even if you say, "I will live completely differently. I will be a preacher in Japan. I will go down to the harbor and take one of those banana ships and leave Norway behind, just go aboard, hide away, and then appear somewhere in Guatemala or Jamaica, and pretend to be somebody else." (This is of course rarely done.)

I have this feeling that the total view is unavoidable and intellectually extremely difficult, but we must have Kierkegaardian disrespect for any kind of established system of thought, any kind of established belief, any kind of established attitude; in every moment you must choose your life, again and again and again. "To hell with everything"—start anew, as if this moment were your first and last.

IV: THE CABIN OF CROSSED STONES

*H*alfway between Oslo and Bergen, the train squeals to a
halt at the tiny hamlet of Ustaoset. It is seven-thirty at
night in the summer, and the sun has just begun its slow descent
toward a midnight set. My friend Leen and I are the only ones to
alight at the station, which is right at the shore of a long lake,
with gentle waves lapping against the shore and the tracks. It is
the first such lake above treeline along the train's route over the
mountains toward the western coast.

The train pulls away — we turn our backs to the lake and look
up at the clouds brushing the summit of Hallingskarvet. My eyes
cast a sweeping gaze up the gentle, ruddy ridges to a small knoll
beneath the final escarpment, where the glacier tore against the
rock like a bread knife, slicing the profile of this benign, beckoning mountain. I'm trying to make out the tiny cottage at the base
of this last cliff. Do I see a candle burning, or is that just a
reflection of the sun? Can we assume the professor is at home?

No one in the city knew his whereabouts for sure, so we
decided to take the risk. It was a five-hour train ride from Oslo,
and now at least a three-hour trudge through swampy tundra,
then a slow ascent over scree to the anchorage on that wind-
blown overlook. Let's hope he's there. Otherwise, it will be a
long march down in the dark.

Leaving the village, we follow sheep paths out into the open
ground. None heads straight for the mountain, but all meander
past fine patches of grass — high priorities for the traveling sheep,

*though not so helpful for those of us concerned with reaching
the cabin before dark. We leave the trail and slog it through the
soakened sedge, and finally reach the snowpacks at the base of
the rise. An unhurried climb up the ancient gray slush; as breathing quickens, our speed decreases. Finally we emerge on the
windward side of the hut. From there it just looks like a pile of
rocks, a cairn, perhaps, marking a point meaningful in some
other age, to some other kind of human race. But on closer
inspection, this is really a huge wall, built to shelter the fragile
cottage from the brutal winter winds. We walk around to the
front door; the house looks dark and uninhabited. What do we
do now? I guess just knock. Da-dum. Silence. Da-dum-dum.
What's that!? A faint sound of padding feet from the back of the
house. The door opens. The familiar grizzled, white-haired grin.
"Well . . . your letter, it was a bit hard to decipher. I wasn't sure
when you were coming, but this is a tremendous surprise. Come,
come in . . . We must finish the conversation we began two years
ago inside here. As I recall, you had some reservations about the
eight points of deep ecology, no? Just a minute, I'll fire up the
primus. You shall have some tea!"*

*It is the summer of 1985. This is the second time I have met
Arne Naess, and our friendship is already set in the manner of a
long, unfinished conversation that starts and stops across the seasons and the continents. We are up at Tvergastein, the mountain
hut that he calls his home, nearly two thousand meters high,
three wet hours uphill from the Ustaoset station.*

*Arne had this place built over fifty years ago, and he has
spent more than ten full years of his life up here. The walls and
shelves are the material memories of his life. Up here, he has carried the most stalwart works of Western scholarship and
tradition—the complete works of Aristotle and Plato, handbooks
of chemistry and physics, the novels of Dostoyevsky, and the letters of Spinoza. Teach-yourself manuals for Rumanian, Icelandic,
and Chinese. The most complete Sanskrit-English dictionaries
available. Buddhist logic, Marxist rhetoric, the complete French
editions of Auguste Comte and Henri Bergson, writings of
Wittgenstein, Freud, Ibsen, and Strindberg. Astronomical guides
to the heavens, multivolume tomes on the wildlife of Norway.
This is a hermitage fully outfitted for the study of philosophy in*

its widest definition, as love of wisdom, in the pure seat of mountain air.

With such a weight of ideas all around, one is never really alone here. The air is too thin for anything to decay. Unfinished manuscripts from the thirties look as if they were left yesterday, while the author went out to gather wood or to fetch water from the canal. There is a stack of postcards from a trip to America in the twenties. There are photographs of famous mountains, drawings by children. A Latin epigraph above a telescope hangs on the wall: "verba vana hic loqui non licet" (vain words are not spoken here).

Tiny vials with a multitude of colored substances line a special series of display shelves: These are the fruits of fifty years of amateur "mountain chemistry" like the concoctions of a child's science kit, carried on by one who held onto curiosity through the prime of life—for fun, not for information. There are generations of forms of rock-climbing equipment, from heavy leather boots and steel pitons to light carabiners and high-tech nylon shoes. There are personal contraptions that only the master understands: kerosene lamps that heat tea and soup at the same time, solar-powered reading lights that work even if the sun doesn't shine for weeks, portable desks that only fit particular chairs when certain people sit in them. A huge picture window overlooks the entire Hardangervidda, where herds of reindeer can be seen crossing the swampland, and the distant mountain, Gausta, comes in and out of view through the haze in the far south. The world evolves as we watch it through the glass. Shadows moving across the hills, light peeking through to change a brown slope to brilliant green. The greatest change is with the clouds, which circle through and around the cottage, blowing through us as we stare at them, making us feel as if we move through the weather, not only gaze at it.

Behind the hut rises the final summit of Hallingskarvet, the breadlike mountain, with an innumerable series of possible routes of ascent, from scrambling to the higher ranks of aided difficulty. There are snowfields to schuss down, boulders to practice climbing on, rivers to divert into canals to bring precious water closer to the cabin's door. Endless ways to see the sun rising and set-

ting, *new vantage points, new angles to notice before the inevitable darkness comes.*

The name "Tvergastein" means "crossed stones," referring to the angled quartz crystals that used to be quite abundant in the rockfalls behind the hut, where snowmelt trickles down under huge fallen boulders into rivulets, which drain into the jewel-drop lake several hundred meters to the west. But I imagine the stones as guides that themselves need to be crossed, in the search for the story of the origin of the philosopher's life up here in the hills. I see Arne running ahead of me, always wanting to be first on any of our journeys: leading the rope, breaking the trail. He is leaping from stone to stone as fast as he can. These stones are the objects and memories we try to mark our lives by. And yet, each is so precariously placed that we need to keep moving to enjoy the climb. Running across the stones. Picking up the flattest stones to rebuild the wall. Moving delicately around the largest stones with hand and foot holds, traversing the great boulders in practice for the true ascent, the climb of life from birth, through meaning, to death. This is why we want to live in the mountains, this is why everything tastes better high up where the air is thin, and this is why we always return here to clarify the range of light we call ideas.

Learning to Love

DR: So when did you build this place?

AN: It was in 1937, fulfilling a dream that came to me when I was ten or eleven, when I climbed up here for the first time. At the top of Hallingskarvet, I felt it was a terrible thing to go down. The only dignified way of life would be to remain on the mountain, not to descend.

DR: Why is that more dignified?

AN: Because from here you have a proper perspective on the human being. The mountain is a symbol of the wide and deep perspective.

DR: You wanted to live in the midst of a symbol?

AN: Yes. This was a crazy idea—the symbol is not the thing! I wanted to live on the material thing out of respect for the symbol. This confusion was nonetheless quite an inspiration. I did all I could to educate myself to love everything here, to achieve the most love: the storms, the tiny flowers, the strong winds, and gray days. It was a program, so to say. And gradually I learned that symbol and reality cannot be separated.

DR: It was an effort to learn to love?

AN: Yes. I made a tremendous effort to love this place, whatever the conditions.

DR: You thought this kind of love might be more sustainable than human love?

AN: Yes. And I never thought of ever having a job, a nine to five job. It was quite ironic that a former professor of mine said I should absolutely apply for his professorship, and then if I didn't want it, I could just get confirmation that I was qualified, and live up here in peace in my hut—writing, thinking, climbing, and skiing.

DR: Money was never an issue?

AN: No, because I imagined that once I had this place, I could live as a poor student forever.

DR: Did it cost much?

AN: No. I got two very good local people to build it. The one who was the principal architect borrowed a horse. Olav Vindegg [Wind-edge] was his name. The plan was to take all the materials in by horse in autumn, on snow. He said it would take fifteen sledges full of supplies, and that would cost very little. Then after a month, Vindegg called me up, saying, "Arne, I have now brought up thirty-two loads, and it is still nowhere near done. Do you still want to go through with this?" And I said, "Go on!" And there were sixty-two loads! It turned out that it was practically impossible to get the sledge all the way up. So he could take just a little at a time. He had worn two horses out. Only the third horse managed. I have a fantastic picture of this. You see, to come up here in the autumn is a terrible thing.

DR: No one had ever thought of building a hut so high up.

AN: Nobody. It was complete craziness.

DR: And once it was built, you tried to be here as much as possible.

AN: Absolutely. But idiotically enough, in the autumn of '39, I was made a full professor, with tremendous responsibilities. I managed to place all my responsibilities, including lectures, from Tuesday evening to before dinner Wednesday. So I could go by train to the mountains Wednesday and come back to the city on Tuesday the following week.

DR: Not bad.

AN: Many people thought I was a kind of artist in living, because I juggled everything so that I could live up here, just enjoying the fantastic view, whereas actually I worked many more hours than my colleagues. I could start at six in the morning and work until ten in the evening all the week through, leaving a few hours each day for climbing or skiing.

DR: Now, you had also gotten married about the same time, 1937?

AN: Yes. Else, my first wife, was a very good climber, and at that time women didn't climb so much in Norway. Yet she was so eager, and her nerves were so good. I had complete confidence that women were just as good as men, if not better, on the rock: In a critical situation, her nerves were just as good as mine, if not better.

DR: When did you meet her?

AN: When I was seven years old. We were in school together all the way up to baccalaureate. So we were very good friends, and then for a short time I was in love with her.

DR: Only a short time?

AN: Yes. Then it went back into friendship. When we married, we were extremely good friends, and she was such a fabulous kind of person that I thought there couldn't be any better choice for a lifetime companion. Love affairs might come and go, but marriage was something else entirely.

DR: So you married someone you weren't in love with?

AN: Well, this did not depress me, as it is very improbable that to be in love would be a guarantee that the marriage would be better than if we married as good friends and companions. I believed in our friendship much more. I experienced love only as a kind of craze: the world's best kind of narcotic, an intoxication—the world's best intoxication, but in the long run completely unsustainable.

DR: Marriage was supposed to be sustainable?

AN: Sustainable, yes. But being in love was completely unsustainable.

DR: So you got married, and you came up to Tvergastein to live.

AN: That was one of the main advantages in getting married, that she could come up here. Three days after marrying, we went up here with all the gifts. We stayed for more than three months, and had storms we had never imagined were possible! At that time, it was a much smaller cottage than it is today—and the walls were just standing up into the air, and when we had the northern wind, the walls would bend so that when we had ink bottles, they would then rush all over the table. The wall was pushing the ink, the table, and the bottles all over. This was February, or March. And it looked as if—yes—the roof separated from the walls here, so you could look out onto the landscape. Hastily, I gathered all heavy things, and loaded down the roof so that it wouldn't collapse. If the roof had lifted just a little more, the wind would have taken all of it. We kept a heap of stones in the middle of the room here, so that if the roof went away, it wouldn't also take away the floor. We would hold onto all those stones, and try to somehow manage to live. The conditions were horrific, and my wife never complained at all. I was crazy. She was not crazy at all. She was quite normal . . .

DR: Do you think this was what she wanted to do? Or was she being nice?

AN: I think that she loved me, and she had decided this was the man she would like to have. And she loved mountains, she even loved climbing, and her integrity as a person was much greater than mine.

DR: Do you often wish you were more integrated?

AN: Yes, I would say so. I've found myself to be a little of everything in a way. I thought that if people lived two or three or four hundred years, in the formative years they could be everything. For instance, they would be torturers, they would be saints, for, let's say, fifty years. Then they would spend a couple of years as murderers, then they would be scientists, then they would be dancers. They would be extremely faithful to one person of the other sex for, let's say, ninety-nine years, and then have ninety-nine partners each of the next ninety-nine . . . Everything. That's what I felt. In every person there are infinite possibilities . . . I was married to Else for ten years, and she was not dominated by me.

DR: No?

AN: Of course, she had so much in common with my way of life, and she willed it so much, that it may have looked like domination, but it was not so, and she didn't like it at all when it was pointed out that she was doing the things I liked. She really liked them, too.

Seeing More in Less

DR: What are some of the strange sensibilities regarding different kinds of life that you've learned at Tvergastein?

AN: If a flower in a botany text is described as being from ten to thirty centimeters tall, you might find the same flower here and it's only five centimeters or a little less. But the flower is complete. I have this feeling that the Self-realization of this flower is only to be five centimeters—and this is just as high. You have here this Arctic gentian in a bad summertime like this one, and it is only one centimeter high, and still a fantastic flower. With regard to human life, I have the feeling that a life at Tvergastein, this extremely barren and so-called empty landscape, may be exactly on the par of a life in the South American jungle. It's a question of what you see and what you don't see, as the human being has an astonishing capacity to grasp an enormous richness of reality.

DR: You like it because of the simplicity of activity amidst a vast range of possibilities.

AN: All the means are simple and the ends are rich.

DR: So you have time to pay attention to things.

AN: I have sat here in the eight-meter-square garden and just tried to count all the thousands of plants that blossom there. The task is endless, and there is no need to wish to finish it.

DR: A microcosm of the country.

AN: A microcosmos, and it is fantastic to see the changes. I have learned an admiration for the minute, to say it very simply: Where others see adversity, I see the Self-realization of tiny beings in nature.

DR: How did this move over into a philosophical focus on ecology and environmental problems?

AN: That should be quite clear. There is a kind of equal status of organisms at extremely different levels of development. You see the tremendous importance of bacteria, or nonvertebrate animals. All these extremely beautiful one-celled animals, they get a prominent place in nature, and not just crocodiles and other spectacular animals. You get to appreciate the ecosystems, and you see yourself as part of these ecosystems. I found a kind of rational basis for this feeling of belonging to this rich world of animals and plants and rocks. Humans do not depend on nature by minding it, trying to dominate more and more and be less dependent; you see the dependence as a plus, because it means an interrelation, whereby you yourself get to be tremendously greater, reaching from macroworld to microworld and back again. Feeling extremely small in the dimensions of the cosmos, you yourself get somehow widened and deeper, and you accept with joy this thing that others might perceive as a duty: to take care of the planet. The care of the planet becomes something joyful and not something that is done merely to survive.

DR: So nature is then important because it enriches the life of the human individual. This is a nature that is important for people?

AN: Yes, but the usefulness for people is one thing. Usefulness for nature is more important. So it is not human-centered, unless you think of humans as infinitely deep . . .

DR: But nature need not be opposed to humanity; concern for nature does not preclude concern for people.

AN: No, it is wrong to place one before the other, because humans are not merely egos, where you have an external world around which is infinitely far away from the human spirit. Get rid of that dualism! Then the term "environmentalism" is meaningless because it implies a very artificial kind of cleavage between humans and everything else. From our individual selves we look out toward the Self of the world.

You Are Competent

AN: Time for a break . . . Ummm, the deep satisfaction of whiskey in my mouth. You have already finished all of yours?

DR: Almost.

AN: Oh, almost, you have any left?

DR: A tiny bit. (Sips)

AN: You are competent.

DR: (Laughs)

Don't Wash Your Dishes!

AN: So this is an example of how tiny things can be so important up here. If we are at the moment engaged in ecological thinking, I might try to use a match twice, and here at Tvergastein I am only satisfied if I can use the same match four times, by extreme dexterity of movement with the kerosene stove. And this then has developed into a kind of game, to be able to use a match many times: four times, and then my wife, Kit Fai, would be able to do it six times. And with a hundred other things. Small, tiny things. This may look completely ridiculous from the outside, of course, but on the other hand it is part of a human kind of life, embracing playfulness.

DR: So it starts out as a game, but there are also these rules for excessive frugality in life up here in the mountains, like never washing your dishes, keeping the temperature not too warm, so you never get too comfortable . . .

AN: That's right, washing dishes is a very complicated affair, because it depends how one treats the dishes. I am glad to say that the biologist Michael Soulé, who lived for many, many years among Buddhist monks, has informed me that when they finish a dish, they first of all get it as clean as possible by eating. Then they take a little water with a spoon, and cleaning it still more, they drink that water, so there will be no waste. Such things are quite amusing, but they do reflect an attitude of ecological concern. One should never of course point it out in a moralizing way, and people who wash and wash and wash — never mind. They have to find out themselves that, for instance, here in Norway, sixty or seventy times as much energy is used in washing up than in any poor country. And *their* dishes are just as clean.

DR: But it's also part of the kind of cult of frugality you've got up here in the mountains.

AN: Yes. But I feel that I live in luxury. Only in the city do I feel stingy.

DR: Never eating more than one square of chocolate at a time. Always saving a little bit more than is necessary, holding back.

AN: That's right. People don't understand. Yes, holding back. That's an old habit, it has to do with what in psychoanalytical circles is called an anal character. This is very common among businesspeople who might defecate irregularly because of the curves of the market, and so on. Holding back has on the whole been a very nice thing for me, because I then have much more pleasure seeing the chocolate still there after I have eaten! But, of course, for certain other people it would be annoying. On the whole, I am glad about that. Here at Tvergastein there is a kind of system. But you may bring your own chocolate and wash your own dish. I won't stop you.

The frugality started also for economic reasons—if I would have no kind of nine to five job, I would need to conserve. I imagined a rich life through simple means. Being rich usually has to do with money and property. But we have many things to enjoy which we might not own or purchase: I look at all the things I have here, and I would say I am immeasurably rich. Especially in winter if I have, let's say, five or six canals where the water froths from the lake all the way up, then to look at those containers, and to look at the wood I have for burning, and so on. All this gives me pleasure, and I see that I am immensely wealthy here.

DR: Let's talk about some of the things you do that make this lifestyle rich. What are some of the things you've most enjoyed in life up here, the ways you've determined to study things that don't require so many means but are done for, say, your own fun, mostly, like the chemistry and the Sanskrit. Could you talk a little about that?

The Study of Complexity

AN: Yes, so far as I can see, it's a great thing in life if you can have a complex day and complex week and complex month. That is to say, you have everything. Friend or wife all the time—love, work, and leisure. In a week you have, of course, all the joys: eating good things that you have carried up yourself, reading a novel, a little mathematics, and some chemistry. Then you go out, doing different kinds of sports: a little climbing, running, gymnastics, so that you have a richness and diversity of activity—no kind of cleavage between work and holiday. The last holiday I had was at school.

DR: But others might say your whole life is a holiday.

AN: Yes, OK, let them say that. Whatever I do has a playful aspect to it. I like to read advanced chemistry books where I don't understand everything. It's nice to do that a little, but then it's even more fun to do experiments, where you cannot see from a textbook what will happen, and you predict what will happen and the opposite happens at least fifty percent of the time. I have made between four hundred and five hundred compounds over the last fifty years, which you see on display all around the hut.

DR: And you weren't necessarily making them to increase scientific knowledge.

AN: Not at all. Nobody in this sophisticated generation would try to make these things in such a simple way. A "real" scientist would use much more energy, much more equipment, and worry much more about it.

DR: So you were trying to do the simplest kind of chemistry purely for your own enjoyment and wonder.

AN: Absolutely. Wonder all the time. Through these four hundred to five hundred compounds, I developed a much keener sense of color: Copper, cobalt, chrome, and certain other elements have wonderful colors. These are the colors used by da Vinci, Velázquez, Rubens, and van Gogh. And when I did very wrong things, I might get two or three colors in the same vessel and it was almost a complete failure chemically, because I couldn't know what they were, these strange substances. I started fifty years ago with this and, of course, during that time, nearly all of these chemicals that I have in very tiny glasses have been changing, so I wonder what is going on over time. There is a hole in the floor and a couple of places in the roof here that are black from some rather innocent mistakes. I don't find it especially interesting to make explosions, I am glad to say.

The variety of chemicals in modern chemistry is so enormous, and I bask in this variety: It's so delightful, because all the different metals are together; you have a feeling of richness, which is not the richness of nature, in the sense that you couldn't possibly find all these substances in nature very easily. You have to purify—these are extremely artificial creations in these small glasses.

This also shows how the life at Tvergastein is a special kind of life; you come to pay great attention to very strange things. When you come here in June or July, and haven't been here since wintertime, and coming from the rich flora at the sea level, up here the first hour you notice nothing at all, but after three weeks, it's as busy as a jungle. And when you return to gardens with tulips and such, they seem so excessive—such enormous things with so little variety, so uniform, almost militaristic. What I am driving at is that human beings have infinite possibilities to live in different worlds, all of them part of reality, with an infinity of variety. It is complex, not complicated—that is to say, composed of meaningful relationships, not confusing ones.

DR: Tell me more about this difference between complexity and complication. It's an important one.

AN: A day here at Tvergastein can comprise everything, and there is a minute, but complex, life, embracing all aspects without too much distraction. And the means are so simple that you are in a completely satisfactory state practically every minute.

DR: Because you're doing so many different things?

AN: Because the means are so simple and they encompass all aspects of life.

DR: So the means have to be simple for something to be complex?

AN: Yes. The more complexity you have in one day, the simpler your means are. You cannot then take a train, or go down to the car and go by means of the car somewhere, to get to the concert, and you get to a place far away to get your children because they are with a divorced wife, and then you go to the studio to do your artistic work, and more, more. This would be too much.

DR: But why isn't that, too, a life of richness and diversity?

AN: Well, you cannot do it in one day. You cannot do it because the means are too complicated. I have them all here at Tvergastein, practically, and it is possible only because of the simplicity of the means. Most people have a few vacations a year. They say, "Now we should have some amusing things," and then they go far away. This costs a lot of money.

DR: Well, how is complexity more than just you saying these are the things I like to do? What if I take the train, the car, and visit my kids? I've enjoyed it. I haven't done anything I didn't want to do. That's a complex life. It's not complicated.

AN: Well, make a list of the things you like to do because you find them meaningful. And if you ask why you like them, why they matter, you get a little further down to more basic interests and needs. And then complication would be where you use so much time and energy on the way to one of these needs that it is impossible to satisfy the others. You have to wait until you get a vacation or until you are in a certain place in the concert hall, or else you cannot get what you need.

The complications in a modern city are quite excessive. You have a typical, ordinary kind of workday, nine to four in Norway or nine to five in the United States. You have a rush hour when you start and a rush hour when you end. You lose if you don't like to drive a car. If you do, of course it's very nice for you, especially if you like traffic. You have friends who live very far from each other. And then you are again in traffic. Let's say you want good music enough so that you do an extra hour of work in order to get income enough to have the sophisticated means for playing music, whereas here in the hut, the way of life is such that I can enjoy these very old Caruso discs, records that are impossible to listen to in ordinary circumstances, because they are so scratched and so on. But you come to accept it. You take a disc from 1935 and you can use it. The music is still able to shine through.

DR: Now, why is it easier to listen to them here?

AN: Because the atmosphere is so pure.

DR: You mean just anything is appreciated. Just the fact that it's there, it's appreciated.

AN: Yes. Water, for instance. Water is appreciated. But it doesn't take a very long time to get more water. We have need of company, of course. There my needs are moderate, so if I have a friend here, it's fabulous, very good. And if I don't, I feel something is missing.

DR: So you don't like to be completely alone up here?

AN: No.

DR: Have you ever liked it?

AN: No, not really.

DR: So you wouldn't want people to think that you're a kind of mountain hermit?

AN: No. If I'm alone, my imagination takes over, and I leave the surface of the earth, in the sense that I forget time. I lose myself too much. I must be drawn back into normality and duration. Climbing can help me with this. I liked climbing and when I was young, that meant spending a lot of money going all the way to the mountains, taking a long time to get there. Here, I can stop working on some philosophical problem and then just go out. And after fifteen minutes walking, I find more than enough climbing.

I have skiing, of course, until July. I have flowers, and then some people are willing to come up here, but not always at the best times, so there is an unsolved problem: how to have very good people here. I need only one at a time. So I would call the complexity here great. But complexity is not everything—no, no. I only say that complexity may be decreasing in the wealthier nations today. The amount of choices is tremendous, but we have fewer reasons to choose. There is more boredom than ever. There are a fantastic number of means not to get bored. But have we really learned how to choose?

Mathematics and God

DR: In a sense, you are returning to an older idea of what the philosopher is: someone who knows the extent, if not the particularities, of knowledge.

AN: Yes, a generalist. I had this joy for mathematics and I had not the slightest care that I was still working in a field that my mathematician colleagues had long since cast by the wayside. Everyone learns the quadratic formula in school; it's like a trick to solve the problems. And for third- and fourth-power equations, there are instead several formulae. Then I heard that all of a sudden going from the fourth power to the fifth power, you cannot use any of the means you had for the simpler equations, and my Norwegian textbook then proved that you couldn't get any general solutions. I just looked at that proof for five minutes, considering it too difficult. I had great joy in saying, "Why in the hell, suddenly at fifth creation, fifth degree, fifth power, does everything break down?"

Well, I borrowed some seventeenth-century works of Euler, and back then, the great mathematicians were really writing extensively—they could use fifty pages for something that today would use two pages. They might write, "Thanks to God that this equation works." All kinds of distractions in between the formulae.

DR: You're attracted to this kind of science that blends mysticism and wonder, like Kepler who blended devotion with his astronomy. We just remember him for his equations, but for him, the stars were a whole mystical revelation of the presence of God.

AN: Yes. But I have not a kind of Keplerian mind. I am attracted to the mysticism within mathematics, so to say, where I need not think of God or the divinity of numbers. One should never let the precision of science wear down the wonder within it.

Today, I think it is the number 3,896th day I am here at Tvergastein—somewhat over ten years. Such a long time? I am amazed by the duration, but also enjoy the precision with which I have recorded it.

Being Oneself in the Distance

DR: How about Sanskrit?

AN: Yes, Sanskrit is very much further away from my own language than English or German, so I could love it without falling sway to rhetoric. When I by chance delved into the heavy Monier-Williams Sanskrit dictionary, I saw an enormous richness of terms and meanings—if a word means "chair" or "hat" or anything, some God would have that name also, and mythology is on every page. The minds of these Brahmins two thousand to three thousand years ago were completely soaked with mythology, and they must have had a tremendously different sense of the power of language than we have today.

DR: Do you wish your mind was more soaked with mythology?

AN: Oh, yes, but I resisted that because of my mother, who was always in love with language.

DR: But she didn't speak Sanskrit. You were safe then.

AN: No. Here, for instance, on page 530, I read "nala, a species of reed, *Amphidonax karka;* a measure of length, a particular form of constellation in which all the planets or stars are grouped in double mansions; name of divine being mentioned with Yama; a deified progenitor." It goes on like this, page after page. I have a lot of time for this kind of thing at Tvergastein. I wrote an introduction to Sanskrit, "Sanskrit for Generalists: A Mild Introduction and Guide by Arne Naess"—specializing in the beautiful philosophical terms.

DR: Who did you expect would use this?

AN: Well, there are about one hundred copies and, let's say, twenty have read it—people who simply derive pleasure from the exploration of new languages. I still know about seven hundred words and very few sentences. But it is purely for fun, whereas ordinary lectures in Sanskrit at Oslo University were fantastically difficult for any other people than the most gifted students. The grammar with 126 rules of beautiful sound—it's such an intriguing whole.

DR: So you were never tempted to get so involved in this so as to master it?

AN: Oh, no, not in the slightest. I mean, it takes years and a young mind. I know a professor now at Berkeley, Fritz Staal, who helps me find easy sentences, but they are still too difficult. Yet, I enjoy listening to the Vedas and other mellifluous Sanskrit texts which are a combination of poetry and prose.

This is a kind of strange planet, and the richness of cultures far away in time and space from the kind of life I have lived and the culture I am in has a great fascination for me. So, all in all, I am an amateur and dilettante, in the old Italian sense.

DR: Amateurs love what they do.

AN: Sure. But it is only idiotic that I don't love the English language, for instance, something practical. It is unfortunately too close to Norwegian.

DR: Do you love the Norwegian language?

AN: No.

DR: Only the distant, only far away things?

AN: The further away and more complex it is, the greater chance I get infatuated with it. The richness and diversity of languages amaze me. In a rich country, why don't many more people engage in activities like I do? One reason is, of course, that in school there is a competition to master subjects in a certain definitive way, and those who become obsessed with one merely beautiful chapter of mathematics and nothing else are looked upon as stupid. You have to go on if you are truly devoted to the material. But I never thought of devoting my life to anything whatsoever.

DR: Except yourself.

AN: No, well, Self-realization . . .

DR: Doing what you want. How different is it from Ibsen's Peer Gynt, whom the troll king advised to "*just* be himself" [vær seg selv *nok*], without thinking of anyone else.

AN: All these things I lose myself in—I get no status from my Sanskrit or my chemistry or anything . . .

DR: But don't you think you always do what you want to do? Just what you want to do?

AN: But that's completely different from being occupied with oneself.

DR: Do you think so?

AN: I am occupied especially with things far away from me. It is as if I want to disappear. That's the starting point of my anti-Cartesian attitude: to overcome the entire subject/object cleavage as an axiom of modern philosophy.

DR: Right. What's your way to get rid of this?

AN: To enmesh yourself in what you are doing, what you experience, in such a way that the relation to your ego disappears, and the Self is expanded into the world.

DR: The way you do these things is a very personal way. Only the way Arne Naess does them. I mean, you're doing chemistry the way nobody else would do chemistry. You're not immersing yourself in knowledge, you're having a good time. You're studying Sanskrit the way nobody else would study it. You're living in a hut the way nobody else would live in a hut.

AN: Oh, I am not that particular. I think that there are thousands and thousands of people who, if they read what I am saying now, would say, "Oh, that's just how I am." But they are rare in a relative sense.

DR: But you like your own peculiar ways. Look at this contraption next to your chair, with tea, and a lamp heating up the soup, and this concentrate. I mean, who else would live this way? This is Arne Naess.

AN: Well, there are others who have their own contraptions. I read, for instance, that Barry Goldwater, the great conservative senator, had a lot of contraptions in his house.

DR: Uh-huh. But he's another person, an individual. That's not getting lost in the thing itself, is it?

AN: Oh, he would probably say that when he uses these contraptions, he would be in these contraptions. He loses his ego and senatorial status and all that, deepening and widening the Self. It's personal only because if you follow the impulses you have, there will be originality.

DR: It's more the method of combining them that's original, the way of working with things. Whether better or worse, it's very special. The way you make tea is unlike anybody else would . . .

AN: (Laughs)

DR: . . . in the Western world and the non-Western world as well.

AN: Perhaps you are right. What I say is that I let things be, I let things go, I put out two completely impossible things together in the same pan. I let things happen because of lack of inhibitions in a certain way. I think people become so inhibited when they find out they are doing strange things. "Oh, I am doing strange things, what's the matter with me?"

Compromising Normality

DR: What are some of your unsolved problems in life?

AN: Well, they're easy to speak of. The question of relations toward other human beings may be the most prominent. There are other issues here at Tvergastein: not interfering too much with the ecosystem, but nevertheless having this pleasant occupation of making canals for water coming down toward the hut. That's not as important as relations toward friends, though.

One very interesting problem is that if you have here normality in my society, I have trouble fitting in. Look at this diagram: Normality is between the marks. And then I am married to somebody who is within the limits of the normal, but look, I am out here:

DR: (Laughs)

AN: I am with a wife or a friend that is here on the left, within normality, and I am here on the right, outside the acceptable limit. So I say, "Let's make a compromise fifty-fifty," and then I find a point here.

DR: Right.

AN: So this compromise, I am glad to say, is within normality.

DR: Still within morality — I mean, normality!

AN: Yes, but then, she may say, "Don't you see you are very near the abnormal?"

DR: Right. Why don't you go further to the left, back toward normality?

AN: Well, that would be the death of me. Even to get a tiny bit closer . . .

The Changing Face toward Home

AN: But between us, you see that I now do not have the general attitude toward Tvergastein that I had the first ten years.

DR: What was the attitude then?

AN: Well, it was one of tremendous enthusiasm, just to get away from the city. Getting somewhere where you had freedom in my sense, and to sit inside a room in a halfway-warm place, with the same fantastic mountain so close by all the time. Whatever I see today in Hallingskarvet, the color of enthusiasm is only a fifth of what it once was.

DR: Why?

AN: Repetition, perhaps. I don't know.

DR: It is no longer so new?

AN: I am not the same fellow. I'm not the same being.

DR: How are you different? You don't do as much climbing?

AN: After so many experiences of being in unregulated environments, I am blasé. You must use that term: blasé. And I am weak. Storms and bad weather are beginning to upset me. One needs a certain toughness up here. I am getting softer; I ask for sunshine, warmth, small waves in the fjords. Less winter, wind, and ice.

DR: But there's much you still love about it.

AN: Oh, yes. Oh, yes.

DR: Are there things better about it? Now that you're older. Are some things better about it now?

AN: Well, I permit myself to use more energy, so that I can have a temperature where you do not have to jump up and down on the floor to keep warm for sixty percent of the time. It used to be worse.

DR: Even just a few years ago.

AN: My first wife would put up with this. But if I got cold—if it was ten degrees Celsius and it was moist because we had been breathing without ventilation—I would do jumping jacks, again and again.

DR: Right.

AN: And the second wife introduced a minimum temperature of fourteen degrees. She had the complete right to say, "Now it is thirteen." And I used to open the window in the wintertime and put my head out into minus ten, still in the night, without wind, just to experience the night outside, being inside in a sense, only the head outside.

DR: And sleeping that way, or just looking?

AN: No. I then closed the window. But I got the stillness. I got a lot of qualities different from seeing through the window by having the head outside.

DR: Of course.

AN: Ridiculous. And I'm saying you have to be ridiculous to some extent if you have certain goals that are always in your mind. You develop ridiculous habits. My third wife, Kit Fai, is even more sensible, so she has even less tolerance for this kind of thing.

DR: But I still want to know if there is anything better about life up here now that you're older?

AN: I said that now I am more tolerant . . .

DR: That's more like an apology. Is there anything better? Have you reached something in your life about which you can say, "Yes, I'm glad I'm here now, and not back there when I was younger"?

AN: Something missed when I was younger?

DR: Yes. Some improvement. For all the readers over ninety years old, you know. Some hope. Anything?

AN: Yes. With old age, the pressures should be much, much less. And especially if you only have a few years left, as with my older brothers, you may experience a kind of existence that is joyful in a mild way, and there is nothing that really excites you in a negative way. Not even the chart of the illnesses you have. Mostly if you are over ninety, you have really three or four illnesses or at least weaknesses, and they only get worse, but you adapt. You get experiences you never could have practically before. You have the sense you are finished. Life as ordinarily conceived is complete, because there are no more pressing goals.

DR: You begin to enjoy and appreciate life in itself. Your own life, instead of this kind of life where you need to accomplish something to reach satisfaction.

Crossing the Stones

AN: Yes. Of course, that is a dangerous formulation, but it is a good formulation. I have heard that people with most of their life behind them feel more satisfied than ever before. They can dwell in this satisfaction without disturbing thoughts, without disturbing thoughts at all. There is an author, an old, old man, who was asked, "Well, what are you still doing?" He said, "Well, sometimes I am sitting and thinking, and sometimes I am just sitting." My God. It's good—sometimes I am just sitting.

Later on in life up at Tvergastein, when I am carried up here on the horse, for instance, my head may turn and you will ask me, "What are you looking at?" and I will say, "I don't know." There is something entirely satisfactory in saying this. There will be the absence of effort, not to think of this or that. All worry is over, and then, we have serenity. That's a good word.

DR: Serenity.

AN: . . . which you couldn't have had before. If you die very fast, it's practically impossible. But if you have a long kind of death, a terminal phase of life, you may adjust to the peace.

DR: Do you think you'd like to die up here?

AN: I don't know. This is where I most belong. In a few years I may change my name to "Arne Tvergastein." But that is, I must say, a bit affected.

DR: And then we can carry you up here.

AN: Yes. And I would look at this, maybe [he picks up a thermos] with more excitement than ever. Perhaps because of a complete lack of concentration. There will be no willpower left, so to say. This thing now was smiling, looking not at me, but out here . . .

DR: The thermos?

AN: It has a big mouth.

DR: Yes.

AN: . . . this part here, and you see it's turning completely this way here, and the direction would be so clear—I am so sure everybody has an immense number of experiences like this which make the environment alive. It would take me six hours to describe just a little of what I see, what I experience.

DR: Experience is such a long word. It seems too analytical already. And by that time, you've already moved onto another experience.

AN: Most of the time we can use the term "see," but then sometimes we must use "experience."

DR: Right. Feel, touch, know, get . . .

AN: Get.

DR: Apprehend?

AN: Also, the motor part of experience is easy to forget. So you get the impression that you see, you are quiet. You do not do anything. But children grasp immediately the use as part of the thing. And you say, "No, let this be." Let this be. The first time they get it into the mouth, of course. "Get" can also be getting down on paper.

DR: Get?

AN: Get it down on paper.

DR: Right. Or on tape . . .

AN: First in the mouth, and then when this child gets to be an author, even in bed with his wife, this can be used . . .

DR: Get it all down, it will all have a place in the work of life.

AN: This can be used, this can be used, this can be used.

DR: This can be used.

V: INSPIRATION AND POSSIBILITY

A rne Naess thus far appears to be a rather self-made man,
*breezing from mountain to city on his own track, taking in
ideas, conducting experiments, assessing all the results on his
own terms. Yet, every thinker has his mentors: those whose life
and work appear exemplary amidst the imprecise surge of time.
For Arne, the two most striking influences in this regard have
been Peter Wessel Zapffe and Baruch Spinoza, the latter as
master heretic and crystalline thinker of the past, and the former
as climbing partner, bard, and cynic, who never failed to enjoy
and make use of life.*

*Peter Wessel Zapffe (1899-1990) was the thorn in the side of
Norwegian philosophy. His talents spanned from law and logic
to storytelling and alpinism, always marked by a peculiarly dark
take on life. He penned his law exam in verse, wrote the systematic philosophy of the sleeping bag, warned of the transformation
of Norway into "Apparatlandschaft," and criticized drama in the
theater and in ordinary life. His massive doctoral thesis, published as* Om det tragiske *(On the tragic), presents his guiding
idea with a weight of examples and defenses. It is a uniquely
Nordic existential view, clearly carved out of seasons where one
faces either dark or light, in extreme, never moderation. The
book deals with tragedy in its greatest sense, where the tragic
hero is the entire human race: Our tragedy is to be the first species to awake and consider our situation on this earth. We study
our surroundings, learn all we can, and reach a somewhat*

depressing final conclusion: The planet, in all its glory, would be better off without us, so we had best abdicate our position as caretaker or conqueror, and quietly let Homo sapiens *dwindle away to join the ranks of the extinct. We will have been a species that has served and done its time, ultimately wise enough to admit defeat when the moment demands it. That moment is now.*

But a tragic figure rarely gives anything up. One feels the catharsis, but learns to go on from it. Zapffe himself lived to the age of ninety-one, all the while carrying on about how we should step back and accept defeat. Yet, one finds a way to revel in the bleak vision, delighting in the new ways self-condemnation can drive us to greater heights. This is how existentialism becomes a tool for mountain climbers: You enjoy the futility of the ascent, however far you have to go, however hopeless the chosen route.

Arne met Zapffe on the climbing cliffs of Kolsås while still very young. The boy was just testing his wings in philosophy, and Zapffe realized he could fly far—if he could accept the irony of it all. Arne was impressed by the older man's ability to describe experience. Here was a rhetorician who was not his mother, so he was able to take it in. An angry man, obsessed with the limits of existence. Arne was never to follow as singular and isolated a path as his, but was bemused that such a dark character could laugh at so much. To see how bad things are, and still be able to smile at them—this is the most solid kind of joy.

It is related to the joy Arne would experience in the throes of systematic philosophy. "We crave such systems," he has written, "and we act as if we know them. But they are impossible." Fascinated by the claims of completeness of the great philosophical systems of the past, Naess also realizes that, although such works may inspire us to no end, their claims to encompass human knowledge in set categories can never be correct. We must accept that there will always be untold possibilities that we cannot predict! Any system's claim to completeness is bound to be wrong, but this does not make it any less serious. On the contrary, the hope is that whatever rules you affirm, you will not forget the direct richness of the world.

This may be why it is Spinoza (1632-77) who has touched Arne the most out of the canon of great philosophers. Here is a man whose ideas were strong enough to get him excommunicated from both Judaism and Christianity, because he advocated a God who was in the world, not apart from it. Refusing professorships as they were offered to him, he led a working man's life, grinding lenses for a living. He wrote his philosophy in the form of geometrical propositions, like the old works of Euclid, where axioms were stated and propositions derived and used to prove other propositions. Everything proceeds step by step, from the Substance that is both God and Nature to the ways in which humanity is tied to natural law—and the ways in which we are free from it. There is an order of nature that we are destined to follow, but we are free to the extent that we choose to pay attention to the intensity and diversity of the world around us. Spinoza asks us to stride toward perfection, a reality that will be a true achievement to reach. When we get there, we will know our direct connection to all things around us. It is an early plea for an ecological vision. Although Spinoza did not talk about the saving of the earth, he knew that the end of human fulfillment would be knowing our true place in the network of relations to a God who is the world around us. And this is the inspiration for ecosophy—a wisdom grounded in attention to the earth.

So the lens maker who dreamed of human attention to nature and the logical poet who laughed as he saw the world he loved be destroyed by human ignorance—these are the greatest influences on Arne Naess, and it is they who led him into philosophy, and out again.

Zapffe: Laughing at Darkness

DR: You often speak of Peter Wessel Zapffe in almost reverential terms, naming him as a mentor of sorts. What is the nature of the effect he has had on you?

AN: I was only a schoolboy when we first climbed together, and he understood that I was already on my way into deep waters in philosophy. He had been practicing law and came back to Oslo to study literature. His own philosophy came out in the tales he told me. I remember his story about the death of one of the best Norwegian climbers, Asbjørn Gunneng. Zapffe went to see the dying Gunneng. He had a very painful, unknown sickness. The parents were very Christian, in a certain sense, and they said, "Our son Asbjørn must meet Christ in perfectly clear consciousness, so we can't give him any painkillers." So they didn't give him any, because medicine would make him confused rather than clear for meeting Christ. The moral indignation of Zapffe was tremendous. He talked about Gunneng, and I immediately realized his deep animosity toward Christianity, and also his notion that, as human beings, even our own bodies can be construed as something meaningless. I might look at my hands and say, "What's this?" as I awake in the morning. So he got me to understand his central question, "Is life worth living or is it a kind of indecent drama with no ultimate meaning?"

Zapffe was living in a very dark room. When we got closer as friends, he gave me gifts and all were black. A very big thing for holding pens and pencils and so on, all painted black. His upbringing had something to do with it, and his sensitivity must have been very great. As I came to consider these problems, I felt that he, who had by then started on tragedy, had a personal philosophy of greater importance than mine. A greater philosophy of life. It was such an important kind of philosophy that I would, for the first and only time in my life, really go through his manuscripts, sentence by sentence, suggesting things, because he must get rid of every sentence that could be considered pathological. There were sentences where one would immediately say, "This man is neurotic." I wanted them out.

DR: But there's a strong connection between great philosophy and pathology. Kierkegaard didn't strike out those sentences. Nietzsche certainly didn't.

AN: No, but the best things in Kierkegaard's philosophy do not reflect neurosis. Also with Nietzsche, the first part of his splendid philosophy does not suggest sickness. And where it does point to pathology, I turn away.

I think people have to get into terrible trouble, like Kierkegaard and Zapffe, with religion. You have to have a terrible time. If things sound "good enough," one hasn't thought seriously enough about them. Zapffe had enough trouble, but as I say, he has a kind of commonsense clarity, combined with terrific experiences of meaninglessness from his infancy—a little too strong, maybe, to be absorbed in a philosophical system. So I said to Zapffe—much later, after I was already a professor, "If you insist on a doctoral thesis, get rid of anything where they can grab you." (He wrote his dissertation in the 1940s, even though he was over fifty himself. That is not so unusual in Norway.) I told him that it should be written completely independent of particular personal experience. And he said yes to that. He completely understood empirical semantics and its moral value. He wrote that there were questions that everyone who considered him- or herself to be a reflective person must take into consideration:

What are the metaphysical requirements of a human being? What kind of meaning? Is it enough to have meaning in life, or should the whole thing have meaning? And Zapffe said it must all have a meaning. It's good to go fishing, to go mountaineering, climbing, and all those things. The human being has a brain such that you can survey life as a whole and ask, "Why? Why life?" And I thought that this, as it is argued by him in his thesis on tragedy, is a great work. You get to know what you stand for and you say yes or no. But I do not return to his work in the way I do to Plato or Spinoza. It is too vast, too singular. It possesses a kind of clarity, preciseness, and definiteness of argumentation that is not sufficiently appealing to the imagination.

DR: And it's quite pessimistic, of course, in the end.

AN: I told him shortly before his death that this view of him as a pessimist is overdone. He put certain requirements on human life, saying, "No, life is not something for humans." And that's not pessimism in the sense that he says, "Must I live? It's nothing for me. When I am at my full concentration, when I am fully aware of what it means, then I see it's nothing for me. But I can, as can other people, compromise with the best in myself and go fishing, and I have a mission to tell humanity that it is beyond our dignity to continue to live." And I wouldn't call that pessimism, just an acceptance of the inevitability of human fate.

Wonder or Resignation?

DR: But you still wouldn't hold to his view in the end, would you?

AN: No, not at all. Because I think it's a great loss if we cannot see the meaning of life as a whole, but it is not that great a loss that I can afford to say no. And I also think that, ultimately, there is a feeling of wonder, not resignation.

I tried to see whether he would agree to that before he got too weak, and he agreed, but, of course, one could say that he was much reduced. I said to him that, if I were on my deathbed and were to die, and then were to wake up with a supremely beautiful voice saying, "Hello, Arne, we have a semester starting soon where we will explain the meaning of life as a whole to people like you and Zapffe. It's a special class for people like you, and it goes over six semesters, but we will eventually explain everything, so you may rest easy," then I would be very astonished. But it is not a logical impossibility.

But Zapffe would probably say, "I don't believe in all this," or "Six semesters? Why not more?" He was like that. I would say, "But you said next semester—couldn't I see some of my friends and my youngest son, Arild? Couldn't I meet him?" The angel would laugh, "Go climbing?! You're not mature enough for this! Come back later." What I was trying to tell Zapffe was that ultimately there is wonder. Life is wonder-ful, full of wonder. I wouldn't be tremendously astonished to be woken by an angel, just pleasantly surprised. Kafka's Gregor Samsa woke up as a big bug. He very soon took that as a fact: I am a bug. There's not much to be said, but how can I get out of bed? And that's something like my reflection were I to wake up as an angel: "Ha! Really! It's like this? What's next, then?"

And I see some people like Spinoza and my son, Arild, who died when he was so young—"Let's go climbing." "I wouldn't say, "Oh, I've been wrong all my life in my philosophy." Not at all, and I wouldn't say, "How could I be so wrong?" No. I would say to the angel, "I didn't believe in your existence at all, of course not, and I didn't have good reason to believe in your existence at all." And the angel would laugh again, "No, you didn't have. You did many wrong things." "Oh, yes, I did." "And you will see Saint Peter." "Of course I will. But I hope to see many others." And I would not expect any Hell.

"Take some semesters again. Eternity. You will learn about eternity." "My God, as a human being, what is eternity? The eternal truth maybe, but not eternal bliss. No thank you." "You don't want to join for another semester?" "Oh, yes, sure. Why not?"

DR: Even with your contempt for school?

AN: "Oh, will it be like a school? Terrible!" "Well, you can be alone, and you can go climbing again and again and again." "I'll come, I'll come." That's how I conceive it. It's a possibility.

DR: Possibilism?

AN: Possibilism would say, "Of course you could wake up like that. Of course it might happen."

So Zapffe, I think as a life philosopher, has done a major thing with his unveiling of the totality of human tragedy. It does not mean that he will ever get to be considered a great philosopher, but he has done something outstanding. To be a great philosopher is not wholly admirable; it has to do with the chances and opportunities of history. But his life philosophy is worth something. Everybody who really thinks he or she is deeply engaged with life and death should go through it. Zapffe is not saying that we could have another kind of life without tragedies, but he's saying "No, thank you" to life as such. It was a very good idea for God to make life, but it was a wrong idea to make it in such a way that humans would eventually appear on the surface of the earth. That's what was wrong. So enough. Goodbye. And, of course, this is an appeal, but it should not be any excuse for pessimism. You either refuse to live or you make a compromise, and you do not get pessimism out of it. You compromise, and you try to get joy out of fishing, out of learning, out of having children in a responsible way, to some extent.

Peter asked the university administration to accept money to finance one lecture every year about the meaning of life. They refused. So he felt an obligation to explain it himself, and that was the start of his big work on tragedy. He was angry: "I'll tell humanity something before I die."

DR: Of course he lasted quite a long time. Ninety-one years.

AN: Yes. He expected not to have a long life. "I'll tell them." That was worthwhile. But, I said, "Don't expect too much." He put out his book on Jesus, *The Prodigal Son*, and expected a tremendous uproar, disputes with the Church and so on, but nothing happened. That was a terrible thing for him. On the contrary, the Christians said it was very well written. And many personal Christians read it and wanted to speak to him, but remained believers just the same.

He had hundreds of stories making fun of Christians. His parents would give a big salmon to somebody who was in the same family, and they asked Peter to present it to them. It was for Christmas and they told him to say, "This is from God." He said instead, "This is from my parents." And then the recipients said, "This is from God. We don't have much to eat. This is a message from God." And he would say, "No, it is only from my parents." "Oh, no. You carried it from your parents, but it is from God." So he said, "Then you don't get the salmon." And he went back with the salmon. This was typical.

His influence was great, but I never believed in him. "Believe" is a very bad word. His philosophy is not my philosophy of life. He was great in his philosophy of life and it was authentic in an existential sense, a very high level of articulation of his life experience. And, as I say, I gladly worked together with him on the manuscript. I had no influence on his philosophy, basically, in any way, and he didn't influence my basic philosophy in any way, except to make much more clear this question of life and death and meaning.

DR: But you gave him a job later, teaching logic.

AN: I tried to press him into the university because he had financial worries and so on, and I thought he would be a marvelous teacher in many ways. Yes, I got him a job. He was willing to accept it.

DR: He wrote a logic textbook, no?

AN: Yes, *The Logical Sandbox*. We agreed that if he was right in his criticisms of my own book on logic, he should write his own. But very few students had a sense of humor like he did, and they found it even more difficult than mine, and very few copies were sold. I found it a very painful situation. Zapffe had thought that we had agreed that we would combine his book and my book, but I felt it was impossible; there was no way of merging the two. He felt that I was very unfriendly in my way of behaving. That seemed to be the thing that made it difficult for us to be together, so for fifteen years I didn't see him and he didn't wish to see me. I wished to see him, but he didn't wish to see me at all. This was one of the most painful occurrences in my life. My sister wrote him, saying that she was sorry about this, that he was against me, and he answered that it was not a question of that but that our paths in life were so different, it was best not to be together. But nobody knows exactly how we could feel that so strongly. So for many years, we didn't speak at all. Only in the last few years of his life did he consent to see me again.

Spinoza: Intuitions of Interconnection

DR: You speak of Zapffe as a strong personal inspiration, but it is Spinoza that you choose out of the history of philosophy as your greatest inspiration. Could you say why?

AN: The person of Spinoza made a tremendous impression when I read the rather idealistic account of his independence, his sovereignty, his being within himself very much, so misunderstood by others. But at the same time, he was very benevolent and tolerant toward people who were not philosophers, living with people who had simple means and simple ways of life. I was also impressed by his determinism, how we are led by our previous experiences or backgrounds and/or biology to make certain decisions.

DR: So you were impressed that Spinoza went against his background?

AN: He went against his background, and it cost him a tremendous amount of suffering, especially to be excommunicated from the Jewish community. And he also didn't look for a professorship; he went his own way, making a living by grinding lenses. That I found very inspiring. He was egocentric in the sense that he was within his system, building his own edifice, but he was not egoistic, he was a very nice person. So he was an idol for me, long before I was twenty years old.

Even now, I often say to myself, "Can this norm or vision be interpreted within a system with a lot of things in common with Spinoza's?" Especially in regard to ecology. Immediately, of course, I remember his famous letter: Imagine you are a tiny worm living in the human bloodstream. How much can you know of the whole that you live within? Only at best how things might be interconnected. He talks about the infinity of beings having an infinity of possible relations. Our mind and body are connected, so that you cannot possibly say that when you are spiritual, you try to avoid bodily temptations. The most fantastic thoughts and actions have a correlate in the body. For instance, in the neck, you have microscopic small movements of the muscles. And if you think, for instance, "Hmm, it's raining." If you think it with more and more emphasis, you feel very soon that your breathing is changed because of muscle movements in the larynx, and therefore there is a correlate also to a thought that is infinitely deeper and more comprehensive than the thought of rain. Spinoza is very good at undermining this cleavage between the spirit and the body, and therefore also between subject and object.

DR: Do you like his equivalence of God and Nature?

AN: There is no equivalence between God and Nature, but he has two concepts, namely *Natura naturans* and *Natura naturata.* That is to say, the creative Nature and the created Nature. He has no name for the whole.

DR: He has *Deus sive Natura*: God or Nature.

AN: Yes, the term "God" is more connected with *Natura naturans* than *Natura naturata,* but it is not equivalent with *Natura naturans,* the creative, because humans participate also in *Natura naturans.* The more free we are, the more we are motivated with the power of *Natura naturans.* So he is not a pantheist, finding God everywhere he looks. I call him a panentheist—that is, the one God is everywhere, and everywhere is in the one God.

DR: But doesn't nature get divided, if it's both *naturans* and *naturata?* Isn't that some kind of schism?

AN: No. They are two aspects of the whole that has no name. It's only a question of aspect—there is nothing, no thing, no entity that is not *Natura naturata*, part of *Natura naturata*, and there is no entity not part of *Natura naturans*. Everything has both a dynamic side, which keeps it changing, and a static side, which allows us to identify it as a thing in the first place. But there is a common feature, an attribute of all living beings. Fundamentally all living beings are one, and we can easily get to a kind of nature mysticism. This is a feeling of unity.

DR: But you yourself have said you wanted to shy away from nature mysticism.

AN: Yes, if it implies that you lose yourself, and there it is important that the third, most important category of knowing in Spinoza is knowing of particular things.

DR: In a direct, intuitive way.

AN: Yes.

DR: Could you say something about that kind of knowledge? When have you felt it?

AN: Well, I was very impressed with the Renaissance doctrine of microcosmos and macrocosmos: that everything mirrors macrocosmos in one way that's very difficult to make precise, but in one way, every little flower as it is one out there would mirror macrocosmos in some way.

DR: How about a piece of a flower?

AN: No. If it's but a fragment, it will not mirror at all.

DR: You mean everything that can be considered a whole in some way reflects the total unity of all things?

AN: Yes, that's right. Therefore, I have this ontology of wholeness, where you have subordinate and superordinate wholes, like a movement within a symphony, partaking in the whole and nevertheless being something in itself. [This is discussed in chapter 8.] It is the same with us: We are something unique and something without which there would be no whole. The whole is dependent on the—I wouldn't say parts—but on the singular beings, and the singular beings are dependent on the whole. It is a so-called internal relation, speaking philosophically, between the particular beings and the whole, so that the definition of you or of me, the so-called essential definition, can't stop with the organism. It is, in a sense, outside the organism.

DR: Out, and onward. . . . So what does it mean to say, "Don't get mystical about Nature!"?

AN: The singular being should never get totally lost in the whole. Spinoza uses this term, "Substance," which can be misunderstood to be something that's only in itself, whereas nothing else is in itself so that we are somehow lost in substance, not in ourselves. People get this from taking Spinoza's geometric logical structure too seriously.

DR: But isn't it the structure that appeals to you?

AN: Not at all. The total system, yes, but not the logical structure.

DR: You mean not the geometric way he explains it?

AN: No, no. No, that, of course, is illusion.

DR: But you have always been impressed by his logic, if not his mechanistic worldview.

AN: I am impressed by the logic as a tool, but it is an extremely abstract tool, and it can be overdone, like in logical empiricism, or Bertrand Russell trying to solve the problems of infinity with symbols. I will pretend that I am not thrown out of essential reflections in philosophy through my predilection for exposing things in terms of relations between premises and conclusion. And logic is essentially that: the relation between premises and conclusion. In philosophy, one makes clear one's premises, and the premises of these premises, all the way down to the ultimate.

DR: Do you find Spinoza's distinctions of *naturans* and *naturata* useful in explaining how the diversity in Nature is held together, propelled, and controlled?

AN: You cannot completely separate the thing from the making of it. There is something in your brain, your rationality distinguished as a subject and an object being manipulated. And it's essential for me to conceive of these things together. Therefore, the *Natura naturans* and *Natura naturata* is not ultimately for me a good distinction. If you think of yourself as creative, the creations and the creative power cannot be separated. Perception is inseparable from ontology. And that leads us away from Spinoza.

From Spinoza to Ecology

DR: Yes, his system is somewhat static.

AN: Understanding is placed against causality. Personally, I find that Spinoza's total view is such that I can derive the essential deep ecology position from it.

DR: Even though he says that animals are just there for us to use?

AN: Yes, but he also says that we are there for animals to use. Exactly on the same level. Only that we have so much power. And he is not distinguishing power from right.

DR: But shouldn't we act, according to him, with our power, and use what we need to use rather than holding back?

AN: Yes. Absolutely. Well, of course. You should not at all hold back.

DR: Doesn't ecology involve a certain amount of holding back?

AN: Not at all, according to Spinoza. Because holding back means coercing ourselves, whereas a particular freedom is connected internally with direct intuition (the third kind of knowledge), and that is loving. Spinoza's intuition cannot be separated from loving. Therefore, you do not inhibit yourself when you kill an animal in a barbarous way. The third kind of knowledge of that animal will not permit you, as a human being, to do it.

DR: What does he say about *using* the world?

AN: You should use everything. He has a utilitarianism, but what is useful is useful for you as a free person, not as a slave, and we are mostly slaves, more or less, or splinters of ourselves, not integrated. So particular emotions take hold of us: hunger, fear. You may act in a barbarous way toward an animal, for instance, because your perspective is completely deranged because of hunger. As soon as you are an integrated person, not being coerced by one single emotion—namely the hunger—you may still kill. But you kill in a way that is only to satisfy vital needs.

DR: But what if someone says, "Well, I've been heating my house with a woodstove for years, but it's too much work. It's so much work, I'm a slave to that stove, I've got to cut all this wood. If they only would build that new hydropower plant on the river nearby and get me electricity, I could heat the house all the time and not be a slave to it. I'd be freer and more active, more real, and more perfect—all according to Spinoza." How would you show that's wrong?

AN: There is nothing wrong with hydroelectric power per se. I had a plan to have a hydroelectric power plant about two hundred feet from here; I can nearly see the place. But because of the terrible movement of ice in May and June, my little plant would just be pushed away. What's getting more and more suspicious is the bigger you make the hydroelectric plant, the more damage can be done.

DR: Doesn't it promise freedom, though?

AN: Yes, certainly, but not if it is big enough to destroy animal life, plant life, and the landscape as a whole.

DR: But for the person who's thinking about how to live more Spinozistically—aren't they getting more freedom, aren't they going to be able to do more?

AN: Yes, technology is essential. We cannot be against it.

DR: But how do you temper technology, according to Spinoza? Because Spinoza seems to be encouraging more and more activity. Couldn't someone use him to justify full-steam-ahead progress?

AN: No, because his goal of activeness is the degree to which you unfold your person as a whole. Activeness requires greater integration. And if you need electricity, it will then be subordinated under the needs of the total personality, and that means that you would not like to support a hydroelectric power plant that would destroy unnecessarily in order to completely satisfy a vital need. So, in this way, we are moderate.

DR: But why couldn't someone use Spinoza to justify developing as much technology as possible? How would you elaborate activeness so that it would require more attention to extensive relations with the world?

AN: Well, in the Spinozistic way of thinking, you have these steps of deepness. Of premises. I would say that the less needed in a definite situation, the closer to the satisfaction of ultimate goals of life. And the more you get of machinery, the more the situation looks like a big machine. The more complicated the machinery you have, the more vulnerable you are. Look at energy from a small power station, where transmission is very easy to repair, and you see the same in war, of course. Where you can have tremendously centralized weapons, then you must build them deep down in the mountains. For instance, if you had a nuclear core there, out in the open practically, they could bomb it.

DR: Like they did down there, at the edge of our view south of here. You know that story? [The Germans' top supply of atomic materials was destroyed by Norwegians near Rjukan during the war.]

AN: Yes. It was a vulnerable installation, because one could go in and destroy it quite easily. Decentralization is a good slogan, as you know, but it can be taken too seriously. A big firm, for instance, may have on the whole people who have greater personal freedom than a small firm, where you have a boss and there are five people under a boss, instead of ten thousand people at the top of the pyramid. It may be. So one must be very careful. And we cannot have millions of villages in the style of Gandhi, because it is impractical. We have to think globally and act globally!

DR: Another slogan.

AN: Yes, one that is eminently compatible with a Spinozistic point of view, where whatever you do, you have a kind of maximum perspective, in space, and also in time.

Death of the System

DR: It seems as if each philosophical system, to the extent to which it claims to be complete, or really represent knowledge, is doomed to fail. There are small insights, parts of it that establish others, but as a whole . . . ?

AN: Almost certain failure. And even a full-fledged system, like Spinoza's. I compare it to an empty coral reef, where the animals have died. But what fantastic structures, these dead coral reefs! And I myself am trying to create a fragment of a Spinozistic system, a system in the atmosphere of Spinoza. But his tremendous construction is largely independent of his particular personal opinions and can be used.

DR: So this is the mark of a successful philosophy?

AN: Yes. Independent of the person and having a language that's tremendously suggestive—whereas, Zapffe, as an existentialist, uses ordinary language in extra-ordinary ways, with great precision, and he doesn't leave much to imagination.

DR: Well, he's a stylist. A writer.

AN: Yes, but he doesn't leave much to the imagination.

DR: Because he's an imaginative writer?

AN: Absolutely. Absolutely. That's interesting. He is imaginative, but as philosophers, we get caught into a rather definite interpretation of the text—whereas with Spinoza, not to speak of Wittgenstein or even Plato, you must add your own insight.

DR: And you can argue about it.

AN: To be a great philosopher seems to imply that you think precisely, but do not explain all the consequences of your ideas. That's what others will do if they have been inspired.

DR: Do you feel you've left a similar legacy? It seems like much of what you talk about today is open to very different interpretations.

AN: I am glad to hear that. Yes, really. But when I discover vagueness, I immediately try to eliminate it. So I would immediately try to be so precise that I couldn't possibly be a great philosopher.

The Last Alley

DR: I have a sense that perhaps you got bored with philosophy a long time ago.

AN: Yes. The first time I got bored was just when I got to be a professor, in 1939, when I gave up behaviorist epistemology, and then I got bored in the late fifties, when I gave up any kind of empiricism. Quine's kind. Any kind. And then I got into possibilism, which is a blind alley.

DR: Another blind alley.

AN: It's a blind alley, but I believe in it, just as I believe in empirical semantics, very much.

DR: Is skepticism a blind alley, too?

AN: That is my fate.

DR: The last alley?

AN: No. I have been skeptical since my infancy.

DR: And you have never escaped it?

AN: No, but anything can still happen at any time. On the way, this feeling that anything might happen. Knut Hamsun has something here. *Landstrykere.* It's one of his books.

DR: Yes, *Wayfarers.*

AN: Yes, picture the Wanderer: Today you are at Tvergastein. Next week, you are with a new friend in a new place, and it ends up being six years, because suddenly, on the way, you fall terribly in love.

DR: I know what you mean.

AN: Anything might happen. Hamsun also blurs what is reality and what's imagination. In imagination, you see, everything is possible, and if you have everything possible, which you have in imagination, then you get into possibilism.

DR: How would you define possibilism exactly?

AN: Well, it's most easily understood as the undermining of probabilism. And probabilism is undermined by examining an idea such as, The sun will rise tomorrow. Then the first thing is to say that, well, there has previously been a tremendous uniformity. We might have bad weather and be unable to see it, but it will be there somewhere on the planet. Some people would say, "Well, there are theories about why, and that's important," but then I say, "Those theories about the sun are based on observation, and this of course involves uncertainty. The theories are never verified or falsified in a special sense. So there's nothing in science that goes against the idea that anything can happen at the next moment." The belief in a rising sun requires a faith that the future will resemble the past.

DR: Probabilism.

AN: Yes. Probabilism. And I can't help disagreeing: There is no real certainty that the future will resemble the past. So if you feel this uncertainty, why should you then pretend that there is no uncertainty? Why should you pretend that probability is nearly truth? There is a tremendous gap between probability 99.999 percent and absolute one hundred percent certainty. There is an enormous difference, because throwing a coin one thousand times heads is just as likely as any other sequence. Then, on time 1,001, tails. The sun does not rise . . .

DR: So you're saying that each possibility has some kind of equal weight?

AN: Each kind of possibility has just the same probability. If you throw it a thousand times, there is a fantastic number of series you can have. And each of them is just as probable as the others, if the laws of nature stay as they are when you toss the coin.

DR: So what is the possibilist response to this, and how can it help you predict the future?

AN: It can't. There is no way out. *Why should you go against the series of accidents?* It makes a psychological impression. After death, I might wake up to the seminar in the sky with my late friend, Peter Zapffe. Even though it is not likely, I will be ready for it. I might wake up to a proof that Spinoza's system is one hundred percent correct, even though I had missed it in my human life.

DR: Expect nothing. Accept everything. Somewhat nihilistic.

AN: Yes. But nevertheless part of a reasonable kind of life, where you put things on the stove, and trust they will be cooked.

DR: Why should I trust the stove?

AN: I trust the food, I trust the water, I trust the wood, I trust all these things. But then, trust is a completely psychological term. My trust is mentally complete. And maybe just because everything is possible, you don't have a tremendous trust for this, and mistrust for that. You have an average level of trust all the time. Anything can happen with your friends in your hut. There are so many possibilities that you give up expecting one more than another.

DR: But sooner or later you must choose between one and all others. And then, where do your criteria come from?

AN: Nowhere. Don't do it! And this is a deep feeling I'm expressing. From infancy.

DR: So, as such, it will never go away.

VI: RESIST TOTALITY!

U pon assuming the duties of full professor in 1939, Arne
Naess set about the task of transforming university education in Norway. Under his influence, students first had to pass
an examination in the general history of ideas, called Examen
philosophicum, before proceeding with their specialized courses
of study. Interdisciplinary cooperation was encouraged, particularly on problems of global importance, defining the direction
our civilization should take at the middle of the century. It is
safe to say that, because of Naess's innovations, the intellectual
Norwegian mood became far more tolerant and wide-ranging, as
well as increasingly wary of any single, total vision to guide
humanity. We need many ways, different schools of thought, and
the opportunity to let our uniquenesses flourish. The world of
the future should admit more possibility, not less.

When the Nazis marched into Oslo in April 1940, all this was
challenged. It was no longer possible for the philosopher to
merely think about these problems. Action was necessary. Arne
Naess soon joined the movement of resistance against the
German occupation, but in his own special manner he main-
tained a certain detachment from the goings-on. Whether trying
to save the students from certain deportation, or interviewing
torturers and traitors after the Allied victory, he had a certain
detachment from the proceedings, as much as a committed
engagement in the problem to be solved. Naess as philosopher is

always able to reflect calmly on the situation, however dark the content.

This also relates to his longtime belief in the effectiveness of Gandhian, nonviolent resistance as a tool in the resolution of conflict. Confront the enemy, but do not assault them! Respect the other side; dare to take them seriously as human beings! Action becomes more deliberate, never without premeditation or direction. The solution of disputes may become more complicated, but one does not act without thinking. Only with this kind of consideration will we learn to fathom the disagreements among people.

It is no surprise that UNESCO looked to Arne Naess after the close of the war for advice on the definition of democracy, on the eve of the Cold War. Who understood the concept better, the East or the West? Naess's answer was, of course, much more complicated than they bargained for. The total, single, simplified vision is rarely correct. A captivating world is bound to admit many interpretations. Reality is more complex, never simply right or wrong. After philosophy, we may end up with more questions than answers, but, we hope, more action than complacency, as well. After all the deliberation, all the resistance, one still needs to make a decision about where to go next.

You Are the Enemy?

DR: How did the coming of World War II affect your contemplative life?

AN: Well, I would say that when the war came, it revealed me as I am. I was at Tvergastein, and I went all the way down to the grocery at Ustaoset about the seventh or eighth of September 1939. I found it indecent to ask if war had broken out. So I just looked at people and listened to what they talked about and I understood that there was another world war.

As you know, nothing much happened here until the next year when Hitler went west to Poland. But life was not changed for me, nothing special happened before the ninth of April 1940. In the night and early morning, the war came to Norway and there was bombing. I saw a bomb fall down not very far from where I lived in Oslo, and I saw a tremendous number of airplanes landing at Fornebu airport. When the Germans came marching to Oslo from Fornebu, children and young people ran into the street looking at the spectacle. And the Germans said, "It's war, we are at war with you. Be careful." And they just looked at them, "Really? War? You are the enemy?" This was a very innocent place, for hundreds of years.

But the war broke down some of the innocence. I went at once to the university, where the students were tremendously excited, using very violent language against the Germans. Immediately, I said, "But this is nothing unusual. It is, in a sense, very trivial. They came during the night. That is how it usually happens—the big nation goes straight through the small one. This is nothing very interesting." I found it mildly exciting, but I reacted against this extreme excitement as usual, as part of my old *Panzercharakter*.

The next night, there were rumors all over that the British would expel the Germans from Oslo by bombing them. So there was a stream of people up to Holmenkollen, where we lived. Following my typically abstract reasoning, I found it implausible that the British would come and bomb Oslo. I had a lecture at quarter past one, and I went against all the people to get to the lecture, and I got there nearly half an hour too late and there was only one lonely student. It was my duty to go to the lecture. This shows that I took this professorship extremely seriously!

DR: How did the professorship change during the Occupation? What was different?

AN: It changed too little, because the Germans believed at first that the university should stay open. It would be much more difficult to subdue the Norwegians if the thousands and thousands of students were loose. Better to have them in the reading rooms, concentrated in Oslo. So they did very little to annoy the university. Gradually, some of us felt that it would be bad for public relations between Norway and the Allies if we had such a good time at the university. We had, somehow, to annoy the Germans so that there would be a kind of fight between the Occupation bureaucracy and the university to show that under Nazism, you couldn't have universities.

I felt the distance of a philosopher reflecting on the situation, less moved by what might happen to my immediate surroundings. What the Japanese were doing in China seemed much more serious than what the Germans were doing to Norway. Many of the pacifists became supporters of military action—most of them really—whereas I found that completely immoral. If they were really pacifists, how could it make any difference that in a particular instance, your country was invaded?

Saving the Students

DR: Were you maintaining a pacifist point of view?

AN: Since 1931, I was influenced by Gandhi, and the war made me much more Gandhian. I found that it was silly to give up truthful communication with the enemy. So from the very beginning of the war, I had a terrible feeling of living in a country where untruth was more and more accepted—lies about the Germans, no attempt to get to the root of the situation. Pacifism was esteemed during the war, but Gandhism was considered very strange—that is to say, Gandhi's idea that we should be militant in our resistance. The pacifists would not take part on the home front. They said, "This is just crazy, wars are crazy; as pacifists, we will have nothing to do with it." The Gandhian attitude would be that you would propagate a militant Gandhian position, defending your positions, but without weapons. But things got worse. At first, the Wehrmacht, the military commanders had the power, but then, gradually, the Nazi party chiefs got more power and the Gestapo started being active. Then the Norwegian Resistance began to be persecuted with greater force. Torture became commonplace.

DR: And you became a part of the Resistance?

AN: Yes, but at first I was reluctant—I was more engaged in having the proper perspective on what was happening, and I was extremely eager to take part in university reform and pedagogical experiments. But in 1942, I started contacting people I guessed were in the Resistance—that was all very secret. And they said, "No, your face is so well known that we cannot use you. It would be too risky." So it was only in 1943 that I got involved, through a branch of the Allied Secret Service, an organization that was not Norwegian but allied with the headquarters of Eisenhower. It was the only really professional intelligence—the top people were spies who were active in the First World War or in between, so even when I was far down in the hierarchy, we got a very mature kind of rules on how to behave, very responsible norms.

DR: What kind of things did you have to do?

AN: In 1943, the Germans got the idea that a lot of illegal work was being done at the university and that it would be better, after all, to send all the students to a concentration camp in Germany.

DR: Thousands of them?

AN: Yes, absolutely all of them, but in a very decent kind of concentration camp, for "re-education." After all, they were Aryans—they were more blonde than the Germans—and it was just a misunderstanding that they were on the wrong side. So they started sending ships to the Norwegian harbors to ship all the students by a sudden bang! bang!, surrounding the university and capturing them all. There was a general in the Wehrmacht who knew of the plan and wanted to stop it. That general, whose name was kept secret even after the war, got in contact with the top people in the Resistance to warn the students. It had to be done immediately. It was a question of twenty-four hours. So one of the leaders of the Resistance movement called me at five o'clock in the morning, saying, "Could you please take the first train down to Majorstua?" And I said, "Why?" And he said, "You will find it serious enough to do as I say."

So I took the first tram downtown, and there was the man approaching me, saying, "You must warn the students in Oslo, wherever they are, and we cannot warn them before half past nine, because the Germans will come at ten o'clock, and if you warn them before that, the Germans will not come, but will wait. And you should then distribute slips of paper saying, 'All students will be caught and shipped to Germany.' They will surround the university at ten o'clock." And the man asked, "Do you have an organization?" And I said, "Yes, eighty persons, but they cannot be contacted as fast as that. No one in the chain knows more than two others. So it's no help." But then he said, "We have other contacts, but they cannot be trusted. You must do it." The only possibility for me was to get hold of seven friends and that was extremely dangerous, not only for me, but also because they knew of each other. But I couldn't say no when he said, "You must do it."

And so I called up my friends and said, "You must meet me," one there, one there, at a distance from each other, because they mustn't know about the others if they were caught and tortured. I had to find out places not too far from Majorstua where they would not see each other, where I could give them the message and some slips, saying that they could only start warning just before half past nine.

They each went to seven different places where there were a lot of students. They handed out the slips. But many students refused to take it seriously. They said, "No, this must be a joke." And then a Nazi student called up the Nazi minister of the Quisling government and asked, "Is this true?" And the minister said, "Oh, no, no, it's absolutely false." They said, "All right, we'll phone Quisling." They phoned Quisling, and he said, "No, I guarantee nothing like that will happen," because he didn't know. But five minutes after ten o'clock, I heard the motorcycles approaching the campus . . . There was a tremendous noise of hundreds of motorcycles surrounding the university, and they caught several thousand students — those who were too busy debating whether this was a hoax or not. They were caught and sent to Germany.

DR: So how many were saved?

AN: Also thousands.

DR: Most of them were saved?

AN: No, I don't think so. The university was closed, of course. I then became more committed to the Resistance, but I was continuing research, spending more time at Tvergastein away from all this. There was no story about what had happened that day involving me. Even now, I think not many people know about it.

You may imagine how I was unable to say, "No, I can't do it." You wouldn't have said no. I had to say yes, but under a completely false assumption that I was really capable of saving the majority. I needed at least eighty people, but I had only seven to help me. Oh, they were splendid, those seven. None of them said no. They behaved very well, just doing it, taking the risk. Some of the students just threw away the slips. You see, it *is* painful to think. They didn't even want to consider the possibility of real danger.

DR: Is thought always painful or just sometimes?

AN: Always. Because by thinking, I mean to get further than you have been. That means rethinking with closer attention, going deeper, and that's what I mean. In school, you learn, for instance, that "Norway is a democracy." Suppose then that it means people are empowered, but what about dictatorships that claim they are also democracies? At this level, it is a very superficial kind of classification. These vague, ambiguous, starting-point formulations are used as sleeping pills: "freedom, democracy," and all these honorific terms. They are tranquilizing slogans. They encourage idle talk, and you don't see the tremendous imperfection of what you have said.

DR: People want to accumulate knowledge, but not work for it, and not be uncertain at the end.

AN: Yes, they take it for granted that Norway and the United States are "free." But that says very little, unless clarified. "Of course Norway is a democracy," most people would answer, without any thought behind it. It is so painful to think, painful to really take things up. At the university, it should be painful and students should learn that mostly we just talk, with practically nothing behind the words.

DR: I've heard it said by some people that you were someone who had a tremendous gift for precise statements about things, an extremely logical mind for understanding the possibilities of things and dividing them up and analyzing very carefully, and then, somewhere along the line, you lost it and you decided to do something different. Do you think this is true?

AN: Yes. First of all, I've fought lack of preciseness in situations where preciseness was needed, and I overdid that to some extent. One colleague said to me, "My daughter came home to dinner and at the table she asked for H_2O instead of water. That's your influence." This influence started at the university, but soon it spread into the schools, through the younger teachers. Eventually, I realized we needed general and imprecise statements much more than I previously thought. I found out that a philosopher is a preacher to some extent, and a preacher must use slogans practically all the time.

DR: So then you got involved in the kind of polemics that you shied away from earlier?

AN: Yes. As a German said to me many years after the war, "You, Naess, and many other Norwegians are incurable world improvers."

DR: Now, how far back do you think that tradition goes in Norway?

AN: Oh, it's not just Norwegian. It is the view from the vantage of a small country. In many big-world issues, we carry very little weight, so we can much more easily say, "The world should be so-and-so." Nobody would object, because we have no power. But if your country has a lot of power, you know that you have to be very careful, because then people say, "All right, do it then." We can say, "The United States should do one thing and the Soviet Union should do another, and we are irresponsible. We can't do it because we are so small." But nations with great responsibility must be very careful. So I can be careless about saying ecology should be so-and-so. We Norwegians can afford much more naïveté. The more powerful politicians will smile and say, "Well, he's Norwegian. He can be Gandhian. We cannot be Gandhians; we have too much at stake."

In the Resistance, it was possible for me to act strongly against the Nazis and at the same time say, "Don't be so untruthful about the Germans." When it went very bad with the Allied forces, there were many more untruths than when it went well.

We must understand diversity of culture, but then you should try to find out the priorities you have in each culture, and still be able to fight while saying, "It was wrong to go into that war." You should retain this strong ability to separate the wrong from the right, while combining that with relative, or better, "relational" thinking. We are all relational beings, and all points of view are always relational.

DR: Which means what exactly?

AN: That you are entitled to say X is wrong, morally, and Y is right, and what you say cannot be said to be invalid or only relative. It is relational in the sense that it relates to a total view.

DR: Your own total view, or the total view?

AN: My own, but my own is ninety percent expression of tradition.

DR: Ninety percent?

AN: Yes, I think so, and then you have ten percent as more or less your individual self. But as a professor, of course, you can borrow from different cultures.

DR: Only as a professor?

AN: No, but as a traveling professor, I have much more occasion to do it—I mean, to study five or ten years about another culture. Luckily, we never got to be as cosmopolitan as it was wished in the twenties, when there was the idea of having one culture all over the planet.

DR: Do you think that was a stronger idea in the twenties than now?

AN: Oh, yes. The great word was that we should be cosmopolitan, without any home country. We should blend the best of all cultures into a unified civilization for the whole earth. Then came Mussolini and Hitler!

DR: But by today, hasn't the world gotten more homogeneous?

AN: Yes, I am sorry to say. But when there are still so many violent politicians around the world and still so much tendency toward war, the cosmopolitan idea is the next best thing. If you get too much stress on cultural diversity and noninterference in Africa and Southeast Asia, where you see terrible brutality, then we may go too far. There must be something in nonviolence that can be a feature of all the cultures. And once again, we are into difficulties.

DR: So does the philosopher always have a danger of being a tourist if he doesn't spend enough time dwelling in the different ways of thinking?

AN: Exactly. Certainly. Especially those who think they know a lot about many other cultures, which is impossible.

Resist the Absolute?

DR: Almost all philosophers think they know something about the absolute, so therefore they think they know about something that applies to all cultures. Is that wrong?

AN: We must be firm in our convictions, but realize that they may change at any time. Your firm moral intuitions can wither away—with absolutist intuitions, you feel never in your life would you think otherwise.

DR: On the other hand, many find it hard to choose what to think after a while. They're not sure what to believe anymore.

AN: No, people give up claiming too much and just follow the streams within their group, their nation, or their tribe. Some people have a certain conviction, so they continue saying things like, "This is wrong," looking into the eyes of the other and not saying, "In my opinion, this is wrong," but saying, "This is wrong." I'm for saying, "This is wrong."

DR: Well, you have to, because you want your judgment to apply to other people than the one calling the shots. You've got to speak from beyond your own situation. People need to talk about each other.

AN: Yes. Sure. And so, during the war and later, I had Christian colleagues who fought against my influence. Professor Eiliv Skard thought it was his duty to fight the kind of education I offered the students—talking not only about God but also about the term "God"—searching for the meaning of the word. From his point of view, he had his duty and learned to fight me indirectly, not face to face. I managed, I remember, after the war, to say to Professor Skard, "You are one of those I dislike most strongly in my life."

DR: Why? What did you dislike about him?

AN: His ways of fighting, his ways of introducing other kinds of textbooks in competition with my textbook, but not directly offering a reason. He brought in irrelevant evidence all the time. He said I had been unfaithful to my wives in public, and so on. And I was then able to say to him what I thought of him, and that was quite all right. We ended up being good friends.

DR: Did you have anything against Christianity?

AN: I liked the Christians of whom I never had the feeling they were Christians.

DR: You liked people to hide their beliefs?

AN: No, but I did not like them to tell me what to believe. If a religious conviction came across in their manner, I was impressed. There I felt: This man is deeply religious, so he will not impose anything on me.

DR: Did you feel for yourself that you needed some kind of code of morality?

AN: Sure, but that was somewhat different from what was expected of me. For instance, to have a false quotation that would make an opponent appear wrongfully stupid was much worse than to be a criminal and rob a bank. Or having an affair with a woman with whom I shouldn't have an affair. My morality was a different morality from what was expected from people who were said to be very serious in their morality. But I never pretended that I would be more than average in my personal conduct, whereas I would be more than average in certain kinds of research conduct and other areas where I had a high level of aspiration.

DR: Which areas were those?

AN: Those having to do with proper conduct toward one's opponents and enemies. Tolerance without giving up strong opinions, with great respect for everybody, including torturers. I had to deal with torturers after the war.

DR: What did you have to do with them after the war?

The Torture Stories

AN: One of my close friends, Ludwig Løvestad, was mistreated enough by the Nazis to be left to die during one night. His mother was dead, but he had a stepmother who loved him more than anything else. Nervous breakdown ensued. The light of her life was gone. And then I heard about others who were just not appearing when the war ended. Parents went to the gates of the concentration camps, expecting to see their sons and daughters. Some never appeared. Nobody knew of their fate. And so they frantically tried to find out where they were. They found out many had been taken by the Gestapo, but nothing more. So I asked Sinding-Larsen, well-known journalist at *Aftenposten*, if they could help fund an institution to find out about missing Norwegian prisoners. And I first heard from five or ten parents, but soon we had made contact with seven hundred. I had then between ten and thirteen helpers who took over the whole thing, because I found it too depressing. You see, many were tortured to death and then tied, for instance, to a rucksack full of stones and dropped into a fjord, so there would be no evidence of torture.

There were so many terrible things. I went with the father of one of my climbing friends to see a Norwegian who had probably tortured his son, my friend, to death. We found the guilty person. We three sat at a small table, looking at each other, more or less stunned. It was a terrible situation. This was his only son.

DR: So what happened?

AN: He admitted that this son was grabbed as a leader of a small group of people, six people who were to be let over the border to Sweden to freedom. The young man was then asked, "Who are those who give you orders in the Resistance movement?" And, of course, he did not answer. Then the suspected torturer recalled, "We beat him up and then suddenly he got violet in his face. He probably had some kind of cyanide pill, and he was dead in a couple of minutes." The father didn't react visibly at all. Well—he was probably crushed, and most of the people we had to deal with were crushed—especially this father, who had a not especially good relationship with his son, so I saw all the guilt feelings and all.

DR: What was your advice in the situation to both people? What reactions were you encouraging in the father and the torturer?

AN: To the torturer, I would talk completely quietly, and then he would say, for instance, "Please, couldn't you arrange that I don't sit any longer alone in a cell?" They would have some kind of wish that they thought I could satisfy, and I said I would try to help.

DR: But did you have any advice in the situation, any perspective that you tried to instill? What were you trying to get out of this encounter between the father and the torturer? What was the purpose of the meeting?

AN: Purpose? To locate the body of his son. It turned out that most parents couldn't sleep, in part because of the uncertainty of what had happened. It was much more important than I ever thought to get absolute certainty. As long as there was no absolute certainty, there were painful thoughts: "Maybe he's in another country. Maybe he was able to go to South America." Or worse: "If he were tortured, what happened to him and how long did he live?" So through these investigations, we almost always found out they were killed, sometimes simply shot. That's OK. We gave them certainty. That was all we could hope for.

DR: Precision and unambiguous knowledge were the main goals of this. You weren't trying to investigate the morality of anything?

AN: No, never.

DR: Was the project a success?

AN: Yes. We solved many hundreds of problems. The parents were very grateful.

DR: Did you have any advice for how people should deal with this tragedy, either those who did these things or those who lost family they loved?

AN: Not much, no. Only that life goes on. This son of yours, what would he think you should do? Not give up your job because of this. Go on in life. Either you wish to go on and live, or you wish to be dead. But you don't wish that strongly enough, so you go on. If you have strong enough feelings, you commit suicide, but if you don't do that and you really feel that you shouldn't, then you go on into life. And this man had a terrible one hour, two hours, ten hours, but that's all. And the torturers said it was good for them to meet someone who was concerned solely with tragedy, and a few of the younger assistant fighters were of the same caliber and said how terrible it was that a Norwegian had tortured one of his own. How terrible that he could do it. But when these people were taken, German or Norwegians, they behaved properly toward us, but then they often broke down, being treated properly and being looked upon as victims who must be in terrible pain.

DR: You wouldn't want people to go on living and forget that this had happened to them, would you?

AN: No, no.

DR: But to continue on while keeping the memory alive.

AN: To go through it, not around it. Never forget it. But no mere retaliation. Do not add suffering to suffering!

DR: So was there any special expertise you felt you had as a philosopher about such extreme human behavior as torture?

AN: I don't know to what extent I had special faculties there, but I belong to those—among which also include certain Christian priests—who cannot judge any human being. We can judge actions, but never the human being. To me, human beings have in a vague sense an infinite value. There is something that calls for respect, even in torturers. So that if the torturers get into prison after the war, and they complained, "We get very bad soup," one could smile and say, "What kind of soup did people get in the German concentration camps?"

But that's not relevant. They have to have a proper soup as others have in prison, according to a Norwegian standard of a soup. One cannot say to somebody else, "You are bad," implying "I am not bad." But you can say, "You have done something worse, as an action that's worse than what I have done." But, you may have had a background and experience in your life such that it would be even much worse if I did the same. If you, as a young Nazi, gave me very bad soup, that's OK (laughs), because with your background, you could have killed me, and instead you go and just give me rotten soup. That's very nice of you.

DR: So you found it basically easy to forgive.

AN: Well, I never use the term "forgive." I don't know what it really means. I don't know what kind of real content it has. There are certain proper ways of behaving, but I don't know what it means to forgive.

I had to do an interview with two men who had mistreated a very good friend of mine. He died alone in a cold cellar. And I find it completely inadequate to say that I forgave them. But I told people that I would have nothing against having one of them, whose last name was Saatvedt, as a secretary. He was crushed by his experience of the war. And he was very intelligent, probably twenty-one years old. He went with the Germans when he was fourteen, fifteen, as a rebel at school. He was a typical anti-person: He hated everything at school, except his German teacher. And so he gradually got into contact with the Gestapo, who made use of him. He was so crushed, he asked me to help him to be shot, but I couldn't have any kind of terrible feeling about him.

DR: Did you have Saatvedt as a secretary?

AN: No. He was shot after one year. And later, after three years, the shooting of traitors stopped, not because they were any less guilty, but because the urge to shoot was less strong.

DR: So were you in favor of the death penalty at the time?

AN: Never.

DR: Did you protest against it? You didn't want him to be shot.

AN: I protested in private, and a couple of times I was in the newspaper on the issue. But that had to do with the Norwegian Supreme Court members. I said to one of them (Ferdinand Schjelderup), who was also a climber, that it was incomprehensible that he could vote for the death sentence. He said that if we didn't introduce a death sentence in 1945, after all, people would have taken the law into their own hands and knifed the traitors on their own. There would have been nights where the people would go into places and try to kill all the quislings. The death sentence after painstaking legal procedures was a bit better. But some people would have to be killed. All in all, they shot about forty people. This had to do with feelings and not with logic.

DR: You would rather that they have to do with logic than with feelings?

AN: No, I would like to have feelings, but not feelings of hatred. And not the feeling that you have to respect the hatred of others. This Supreme Court member seemed to respect the hatred of the Norwegian people. And I didn't think that hate should be so respected.

DR: Not since the Viking times.

Defining Democracy

DR: And after the war?

AN: In 1948, I was invited by UNESCO to be scientific leader on a project on the controversy between East and West regarding the definition of democracy. This was at the beginning of the Cold War. So I went to Paris, taking with me one of my gifted students, Stein Rokkan. There were six hundred people engaged at UNESCO at that time.

It was a madhouse, in my opinion. I asked for seven months of study on the meaning of democracy. The Soviets and the Eastern bloc were saying, "We are democratic," because according to the usage established with the French Revolution, or any revolution, democracy means that those who are underprivileged and downtrodden get the power and they kick out those in power. That is democracy. And the West said, "No, that has nothing to do with democracy. Democracy means a government of the people by the people for the people, in which all are given fair representation." Byrnes and certain other theorists of democracy were then trying to clarify the matter, and Rokkan, who has a tremendous ability to read, ordered books and books. After only one week, we had the administrative bosses saying, "Hurry up, hurry up! We don't have much time." They were more and more frantic. They were not ready for something on the level of political philosophy. They would have preferred a questionnaire, so we made them a tremendous questionnaire.

DR: For whom to fill out?

AN: We thought that politicians, as well as professors of political theory, would participate, from all over the world. And we sent it eventually to four hundred people, asking them what they thought democracy meant. And because Rokkan was such a wonderful so-called assistant, people responded. I was really in charge of the questionnaire and so on, but he was in charge of carrying it out. So we got a lot of young, very promising people in the United States and other places, later great names in political science. The Americans were most compliant in responding to our questionnaire. East of Eden, practically no answers at all. Very bad. And in the United States, they did it because they had a great respect for UNESCO. Not any more. But nevertheless, the bosses then told us, "Now you are permitted to give money out for certain experts to convene in Paris and discuss it."

And we picked out people who we wanted to invite, and the national commissions of UNESCO said, "No, no, no." Because we'd picked out very strange, gifted, controversial people. The administrators were beyond themselves again. And I was, of course, much more thinking about the trip to Afghanistan and the Himalaya, the trip I would make as soon as I could get hold of the tremendous money I was to be paid by UNESCO. Stein and I wrote the book together. And my name was never mentioned, because I was a full member of the Paris UNESCO center. Stein and Richard McKeon issued the book: *Democracy in a*

World of Tensions. And McKeon was a kind of fog-king, king of fogs, in philosophy.

DR: Nearly impossible to understand.

AN: And it went very well. Even if it mentioned that the Russian use of the term was much older than the French Revolution. It was sold out immediately. UNESCO was then criticized from all directions.

DR: (Laughing) Nobody liked it.

AN: National commissions did not approve. So they didn't dare give again a second edition. But it is a very good book, revealing the vast vagueness and ambiguity of a central term of our time.

DR: So, in the end, do you think democracy has a clear meaning, of any kind?

AN: No, no. Years later, I got a telegram. From Geneva, some high-level, highbrow conference: PROFESSOR NAESS, WE KNOW YOU'RE AN EXPERT ON THE CONCEPT OF DEMOCRACY. PLEASE SEND US BACK THE CORRECT DEFINITION? I didn't answer. It depressed me so much. They did not understand that a single slogan like "Democracy!" is a sleeping pill.

DR: A tranquilizer. Another vague term that's got followers.

AN: Yes, but it's politically quite important. Of course I'm *for* democracy.

DR: It's like being for the environment today. Everybody is.

AN: Exactly. Certain words are said, again and again. But the "depth of intention" behind them is often not very great.

Gandhi and Galtung

DR: Now, at the same time, you were doing more work on Gandhi?

AN: Yes, sure, with Johan Galtung, now famous for his work in peace research. I met him when he was a schoolboy, when he was doing chemistry. He gave me his chemical stuff, some very nice crystals I think I have still at Tvergastein. He turned out very soon to be extremely fast and gifted, very quick thinking and fantastic in articulation. We met in Gandhism and we wrote books together. For a couple of years, he believed even more than I that you could use logical empiricism seriously in research on social problems.

DR: In a way he really is a disciple of yours, because he's taken the logic that you use and applied it to completely illogical systems in the world and made them all look so logical—he makes such consistent diagrams. When you draw a diagram, it tends to dissipate into space, with no conclusion, totally abstract, whereas Johan's would be sort of complete and everything would fit in and you read it and say, "Yes, yes, how neat it all is."

AN: He was always very quick in whatever he was writing. But one might say that if you have that facility of grasping things and that facility of writing, this can make you go faster than you should. His intellectual brilliance then gets a little aggressive.

But he remains a very strong Gandhian. I think in a modern industrial society, it is nonviolent communication that's fabulously important. It is a kind of violence when you influence people in certain directions without their knowing it, as you do through advertising.

DR: Is this a kind of systemic violence, as Johan might call it?

AN: It's systemic, certainly. That's an important notion, but it can be carried too far when you say that such and such society is violent, because there is a kind of conformity.

DR: Was it important to your development, working with Johan? Was he an influence on you, or did you have more an effect on him?

AN: He had so much talent in articulation that he could win anything, right or wrong. He could do obviously important things out of the head, like this, through articulation. He had not enough struggle, and it is difficult to go very deep if you do not struggle.

DR: So you felt you were struggling more?

AN: Yes. I was struggling more than he did, but as I say, articulation is such a fundamental thing. It's a terrible weapon to have this ability to articulate negatively about people. You cannot forget what was said. We can laugh, but if you don't get to know the person very well, you stick to that idea to the death, whereas if you get to know the person deeply, you can get rid of it. But who knows who? Today, one may have two hundred contacts, and mostly just from what others say about them.

My standard example is Gandhi, the first time he was called on the carpet to have a talk with the top British military and administrative people: "Well, Gandhi, it is a terrible problem. What is your solution?" And he looks into the eyes of this person and says, "Leave India." The way it is said is the absolute negation of arrogance, but it is the way it is said, looking into the eyes directly, and not saying "I think you should leave" or "I think . . ." or "In my opinion . . . ," but just "Leave India." That is nonviolence in communication, in spite of any presumption of arrogance. By his body language, you see that it would have been dishonest for him to say anything else. And so they started more particular things about what could be done, and so on. They would say, "What about the fact that your nonviolence leads to violence?" And Gandhi would have to say, "Yes, that is the most depressing thing of all." So you see, my early suspicion of language made it easier for me to be nonviolent in communication. I imagine I understand Gandhi very well. But I don't know how I would be able to behave in physically terrible situations.

DR: You've never had to try.

AN: No. This is jumping a little in time, but the greatest direct action in Norwegian ecological questions was in the Arctic, at Alta. In 1979, I think, a ship came from the south of Norway with six hundred police to add to the local police. I had the privilege to stay overnight with the leadership of the action. We were all in one room. Lenin, Stalin, and Marx were all hotly debated—all the leaders were former members of the Communist party. One of the most violent kinds of communication there has been in the history of Europe was the Marxist way of polemics and the Marxist way of talking!

But the local population was split in two. The dominating people were against the hydroelectric project. There were a strong minority who were for having this kind of electric power. And they then came and were tremendously angry at us. I was not active in preaching anything, but my Gandhian norm there was that if people spoke to you like this, "What do you mean by this? What do you mean by this idiotic thing?", the first thing to say was, "Come and sit down and have a cup of coffee." And in Norwegian culture, that is a very important thing, that cup of coffee. It is very difficult to say, "No coffee!" It's practically impossible to say "No coffee," especially in northern Norway. So they would sit down and they would listen to the attacks, and they would start saying what they thought and why they were there, and so on.

And where we knew that farmers were against us, we would ask them, "Is there any way we can help you on the farm, with fencing and so on?" And that was the norm in the local population—if you could do something, do it. This is part of communication. You have to do something for and in the community so that when they see you, they have a kind of trust. Only then can you tell them something, say something they wouldn't like. If you do not show solidarity with them, you have no right to go and say tough things against what they consider to be their interests.

A norm to guide action is an imperative. You get shaken: "Enough about your values—now, make the decision!" Well, I value so many things, and so on. Right or left! Then you get a normative system and you feel like Kierkegaard, where you are always deep in the water—sixty thousand fathoms, in the sense that a decision *must* be made. That is existentialism at its best. No more talk now, you go left or right. And then you have to have a proclamation ending with an exclamation mark. You must act! You can't get away from it. That is Kierkegaard at his best. I have been very much influenced by Kierkegaard.

DR: But not his style.

AN: No, no. He is both intellectual and poetic, deadly serious and endlessly witty—a brilliant writer. But his point is fundamental for me: Wherever you are, in whatever situation, you make a choice that is fundamental.

Life Is Like Downhill Skiing

DR: Once, didn't you get elected to political office, by accident?

AN: Yes. They had a new idea that we should vote not for parties, but for individuals off a list in the county of Oslo. And I got the most votes for a certain local position . . . I don't know how. But at least it was a very responsible post.

DR: When was this?

AN: I don't know. I said, "I can't." At the first meeting, I said, "I'm sorry, but I'm not the right man. I cannot support the city of Oslo." What I meant was that I wanted to build down Oslo, and all the rest were trying to build up Oslo. I would devastate Oslo.

DR: How did you get out of it?

AN: By just saying I couldn't be there.

DR: Do you prefer to be on the sidelines of responsibility? Out of the thickets and into the clearing . . .

AN: Yes. Quickest escape route from responsibility, please. That is what I like, but sometimes it is impossible. I was very responsible with all these problems of who we should have as teachers, teaching assistants, and how they should work together. I had a lot of responsibilities, which I took seriously but disliked tremendously.

DR: You must choose the right paths to solve each problem.

AN: Yes, choice is fundamental. You are caught as a human being. In a certain sense, it is dreadful, especially for people who are morally extremely serious—they cannot accept that you go right instead of left without a complete justification. You jump right, and there's a risk that it was completely wrong of you, that it was one of the worst things you've ever done in your life. That they cannot stand. They must have a complete reason and stick to that.

This is the picture I have of life—I said that to my fellow philosophers once: "Life for me is like downhill skiing, when you ski the mountain and you have wide possibilities of going left or right on this nice mountain, and then you have the treeline, where the trees get thicker and thicker and you are heading toward them, faster and faster. Sooner or later, you have to make decisions that are completely unjustifiable. You have a tree coming toward you, straight in front of you, and you have to go right or left. You must make a decision, because to go straight is not a smart thing. You have to go to the left, or to the right."

DR: And you can't do both. There would be very unfortunate results.

AN: You can't do both. And you can't see quite what's on the right-hand side or what's on the left-hand side. Someone in the audience responded, "How dreadful!"

DR: You must act without knowing.

AN: You have half a second and you have to decide. And you think it looks a little better on the left, so you go left, and then you have a new tree and it gets thicker. That's life. It gets thicker when you get more responsibilities, so responsibility is what's a terrible thing for me. They say I dislike responsibility to a great extent. But it's like getting into thicker and thicker forests—if I had been more successful in arranging the university as I liked, I would have had a tremendous responsibility, and there would have been conflicts, misunderstandings, bad lawyers, bad mathematicians, and so on. I am, in a sense, glad that I didn't succeed, that they looked at me to some extent as an enfant terrible. They didn't take me all that seriously. I would get into this thickness with great speed, where I would have to react more and more wildly, with less and less justification. But a couple of my colleagues, like Ragnar Frisch who won the Nobel Prize—he was completely cool about responsibility. He was making Norway into a planned economy. He had a tremendous influence with his economic theory. And he never had any bad nights because of his responsibility. None at all.

DR: Do you feel you've had to work for your independence? Was it an achievement?

AN: No. But it is a kind of achievement to maintain it where it is very tempting to give it up: In thinking. There have been situations where it has been very tempting to rely on the reasoning of others. So that might be a little achievement to stick to my own views. But this gets back to my *Panzercharakter* and my feeling that everything is at a distance from me: "So this fellow is the great Plato? So what? What he says has to go through my modest brain." And if I say, "This is wrong," I would read it once more and again, and I do not have the intellect enough to see the depth, and I am very stupid compared to Plato, but this is wrong according to me. I cannot say, "He is right, just because he is a genius. Try to make me understand! Please try, but . . . each bird sings with his own beak, and I am singing with my own beak, and that's not a very clever beak." I do find many people who seem to be very much more intelligent than I, no comparison, but sometimes it doesn't seem to help them.

VII: DEFINING THE DEEP

*A*rne Naess is today best known for his invention of the
term "deep ecology"—a philosophy of environmentalism
that encourages us to ask basic questions about the place of our
species in nature, in the hopes that deeper questioning will lead
to more profound solutions to the growing environmental crisis
faced today.

Beyond this, the phrase has been twisted in many different
directions. I remember when I first tried to get Arne to explain
more about it. We were climbing the cliffs above Tvergastein, at
opposite ends of an old, but trusted, rope: "So what if nature
has value in itself? How would more respect for nature change
the way our society treats it?" These questions were slipping
through my mind as my feet were slipping on rotten rock. Arne
pulled tautly on the rope, rather than answer.

Over the years, I have tried to get him to comment on the
way this designation, introduced in a five-page article in the journal Inquiry in 1973, came to be taken up as a banner for diverse
ecomovements across the globe. "Shallow ecology" fights against
pollution in the wealthy countries alone, while "deep ecology"
looks for the fundamental roots of ecoproblems in the structure
of societies and cultures around the world. The philosophy
behind the words remains suggestive, not definitive, but people
who take it on don't seem to mind. Arne cautions us to distinguish between the deep ecology philosophy and the deep ecology
movement. A movement can be inspired by slogans and touch

millions. A philosophy is something else again — it's a path of questioning, a discipline that does not gain adherents, but a method that sets thinkers out onto their own, diverse routes. Ascending the same mountain perhaps, but choosing the way most appropriate for each individual climber.

Deep ecology has become an attractive phrase for many people, who tend to bend the term to their needs without bothering to learn what it was originally meant to imply. There are those who use the term to label themselves the real, bold, and serious environmentalists, opposing their chosen few to the vast majority of weak reformist thinkers, who they deem to call "shallow." And there are others who use "deep" simply as a substitute for "radical," which leads their opponents to criticize them for being far "off the deep end" in respect to real problems and workable solutions.

Because the word has been twisted and turned in so many directions without agreement, I feel I need to tie some strands of the rope together here. If deep ecology is to be of any use to environmentalists, it will not be in its convenience as a name for extremism, but as a signal for us to question the foundation of our concern, asking us to articulate why we believe what we do about the singular importance of nature, and helping us to determine what basic changes in society are most worth fighting for to realize the goal of a sustainable world, where humanity thinks of more than its own welfare. It should not be a pose, but a tool to gradually make the viable routes appear in our gaze.

When it comes time to describe the organizing features of the movement, Naess tends to cite the eight points of deep ecology, developed in collaboration with George Sessions in Death Valley in 1984, subject to periodic revision each season. Here is what I think is the latest version:

1. The flourishing of human and nonhuman living beings has intrinsic worth. The worth of nonhuman beings is independent of their usefulness for human purposes.
2. Richness and diversity of life forms on earth, including forms of human cultures, have intrinsic worth.
3. Humans have no right to reduce this richness and diversity, except to satisfy vital needs.

4. The flourishing of human life and cultures is compatible with a substantially smaller human population.

5. Present human interference with the nonhuman world is excessive, and the situation is worsening.

6. The foregoing points indicate that changes are necessary in the dominant way humans until now have behaved in their relation to the earth as a whole. The changes will, in a fundamental manner, affect political, social, technological, economic, and ideological structures.

7. The ideological change in the rich countries will mainly be that of increased appreciation of life quality rather than high material standard of living, in this way preparing a global state of ecologically sustainable development.

8. Those who subscribe to the foregoing points have an obligation, directly or indirectly, to try to implement the necessary changes by nonviolent means.

This platform of the deep ecology movement is to be taken not as a dogmatic pronouncement, but as a starting point to help focus our thinking. It is meant as a challenge to our conventional wisdom, to help us understand our own emotions and actions in the face of an environment that is rapidly deteriorating. Although some find it easy to go along with the list, others are troubled by the imperative that the world's human population must be drastically reduced. They ask, "How will we do it?" and are dissatisfied with deep ecologists' inability to come up with a realistic response. Others feel that deep ecology lays too much weight on the preservation of nature as a separate entity from human society, where they should instead perceive social problems that lead to the degradation of the earth. These "social ecologists" see environmental problems as symptomatic of social ones, and look more carefully at social reform, and less at respect for nature.

The value of deep ecology can only be assessed by considering how it has inspired some to change the way they live. It has changed the way environmental protests are conducted: A nature with value in itself is worthy of preservation for itself, and this has led to the practice of ecodefense—trees may not be able to grow spikes to save themselves, but we can help them out a little.

In the United States, the Earth First! movement has defended its nonviolent actions against the Forest Service and the lumber companies on the principle that humans should not always be considered first. But neither can people be ignored. Looking for the deep social roots of ecological problems also involves the proposal of deep solutions that are both profound and realistic: It is no longer enough to attack unnecessary, gigantic freeway projects on ecological grounds alone. We need to prepare thorough, well-researched recommendations for alternative transportation that will save money (satisfying economists), be locally manageable (satisfying the people most directly affected by the project), and fit into an integrated vision of a viable society for the many different communities it will serve.

Scientists, long influenced by a self-imposed taboo against involving ethics in their pursuit of abstract truth, have finally begun to come around and realize that their work is deeply entwined in a system of values, which they should use their expertise to articulate. The new field of conservation biology has been created by ecologists and naturalists who are not afraid of voicing the moral conviction behind their study of the world's life forms: preserve the diversity of life on the planet! Then, they take up the scientific challenges of determining how much diversity is needed and how we may ensure it by the appropriate natural reserves and proper contact with the diverse human cultures who have lived successfully among the thousands of endangered plant and animal species. Conservation biologists have helped to plan national parks from the Amazon to the Sahara.

Any thoughtful environmentalism leads quickly to a paradox: If there is a sense in which nature is more important than human aspirations, how do we protect this aspect of nature without deprecating our situation as human beings? Human society today changes at an alarming rate. We do not want to deny it progress as much as redefine progress. A return to any self-conscious and romantic past will not work.

Deep ecology dares to hope for a way beyond this paradox. It does not pronounce that wild animals are more important than people, or that breathing in the scent of new pine needles will somehow solve the injustices of capitalist and socialist systems alike. No one should be so naïve as to simplify it into such empty claims. If deep ecology seems too vague, it is because we have failed to catch its spark as a reassuring guide to connect a fundamental reverence for the earth with a need to act immediately and practically to save it. It is a tentative beginning, not a finished solution.

There are those who say that deep ecology is unnecessarily centered around the confining concept of the "Self." Arne Naess tends to talk about the widening of individual concern, not dwelling on the social constraint of thought and act. Of course the intricacies of the world cannot be explained away by the experiences of individuals alone. But as a practical approach to the ecological problems of today, we need to inspire and touch individuals before we can speak of the behavior of social groups. Naess speaks of "Self-realization" to explain the way in which nature is not in conflict with us. We become our fullest selves when we empathize with the world in its widest sense, when we feel compassion for the near and far reaches of the natural world, when we recognize this feeling and are not afraid of it.

Immanuel Kant revolutionized ethics by suggesting that we never use another person merely as a means to an end, but also as an end in him- or herself. Deep ecology suggests that we should never use any living being or aspect of the living world as merely a means to an end. All life has intrinsic value, and this should hold beneath all our own actions and manipulations. This does not suggest that nature is something to be left alone, but only that we are entitled to change it only when we realize its value. As we empathize with more of the natural world, we improve ourselves and our lives.

Reexamining the boundaries of the natural and the human has considerable consequences for all ethical and political theories and practices. Some immediate specifics to be transformed may be the way we argue points in environmental debate, or the way laws are structured and defended. It would be a tremendous step if development projects were halted if they damaged not just a single, individual endangered species, but whole ecosystems whose value could be determined by assessing the uniqueness of the specific interweaving of natural and human history that characterizes places important to us. A reconsideration of values that could be agreed upon by a majority of the population could *result in a reallocation of a nation's resources toward different priorities than at present. The conservation of natural resources leads to the consideration of cultural resources, and we will be driven to define our own human identity more clearly in the shadow of the world's. Here the boundaries between ourselves and the environment break down, and each side makes sense only as it takes account of the other.*

We see how Arne's growing concern with ecology stems from his lifelong love of mountains and other wild places, blended with his firm belief that philosophy can help to solve real world problems. If, at the end, you feel you are still not sure what deep ecology means, congratulations: You are among the majority. It remains a tentative, though tantalizing, label. If it inspires you to ask more questions, you are on the right track, doing just what Arne would have you do. If one honestly upholds that a deep respect for the earth implies a need to work on behalf of our planet, then it is hard to denounce deep ecology. By putting forth the right questions, it may enable us to reconcile our human path with the rhythm of a nature with which we are inextricably bound. This is why, when people ask me, "What do you think of deep ecology?" I tend to respond with a paraphrase of our old friend Gandhi's response to the question, "What do you think of Western civilization?"—"I think it would be a good idea."

In the following dialogue, I press Arne to go beyond this tentative and beguiling "good idea," aiming to anticipate the objections the skeptical inquirer will have. We will see if his answers are adequate.

Who Started It?

DR: OK, now to the deep ecology movement. How did you get involved? How did you come to be called the originator of this movement?

AN: Well, this question is very flattering, and I won't stop you immediately. I may have coined the terminology, and the distinction of a deep/shallow ecological movement, but the originator in our time is, of course, Rachel Carson. Although I had lived in nature all my life, I didn't hear of her until 1967.

I was in the desert in the United States, and my student and friend Jon Wetlesen said, "There is something happening. There is an author, Rachel Carson, who has made a lot of noise about pesticides, and now there is a great movement for eliminating the worst toxic materials that they use, and it seems that this is something you would very much like." I got hold of some literature on this, and said, "Eureka, I have found it." At last, there was a real possibility of fighting to save free nature and to save the planet.

DR: This is something you had wanted to say before?

AN: Eminent writers like Peter Wessel Zapffe had said very radical things in this direction long ago, but he wrote in such a way that people said, "Oh, how well written, how fantastic, this is marvelous." But nobody did anything. Back in 1945, I had joined the Norwegian Mountain Touring Association (DNT) in order to do something different for our wilderness areas. But the more I talked, the less their board of directors listened. I saw there was no possibility of fighting for what I would like to fight for: giving up the really big huts that looked like hotels in favor of small huts, giving up expansion, and being more active in protecting the diminishing wild lands.

I think I am to some extent a coward when it comes to fighting with people. Why did I never "raise hell"? Courageous among rocks, timid among men? I never slam my hand on the table. If I had done that, I'm sure they would have listened very attentively and I could have really accomplished something, but I was just resigned to my strange views, alone.

Then, of course, I got involved in the late sixties, joining people like my student Sigmund Kvaløy. He started a loose but strongly activist organization called (snm): the Ring of Ecopolitical Cooperation. It was the time of the student "revolution," and neo-Marxism and the Frankfurt School were obligatory reading for all bright students. I was a member of (snm), but I never took part in the real work to organize direct action on the great scale like Sigmund and half a dozen others, most of them not committed Marxists.

DR: Why didn't you participate?

AN: First of all, I was then heavily engaged in theoretical work, and I would have liked to join them in some of the direct actions, but I have a very limited tolerance for meetings. And in order to really do the work there, you had to be in a really long series of meetings, talking and talking and talking, and that was impossible for me. I've never been able to do that. Never.

Sigmund Kvaløy had his own variety of Marx-influenced theory, where the concept of work has a very central place. And as a farm boy, he was also very much engaged in the primary activity of agriculture, close to the land. So we differed very much in theory, but completely agreed in all matters of practice, and especially on the high-level Gandhian approach. I would say a very high Gandhian level of nonviolence.

DR: Now you are playing down your role in certain nonviolent actions at this time, but it was sort of taken up very much by the press that you, Professor Naess, were the most prominent figure in the movement.

AN: Yes, yes. That's right. That's unfortunate, because those who worked night and day organizing direct actions were less well known, I am sorry to say, as well as believing in a nonhierarchical kind of organization without single leaders. But the press wanted to identify leaders, and they decided that I was one of the major leaders.

The Contribution of Philosophy

DR: So as a philosopher, what do you think your role is in the global environmental movement? Since you are not a specialist on specific problems, how do you see your function?

AN: It is the articulation of the basic norms within the ecological movement and an application of my analytical training to talk in a bureaucratic way. Not to inspire, show style, or be poetic. I leave that to the artists.

DR: But do you think it's really bureaucratic? I mean, can the politicians make much sense of what you say?

AN: I learned early on that when I get very serious, I talk in the language of bureaucrats rather than the language of fighters in a social movement. I would never be good at facing people and fighting it out, so to say. I can face avalanches, but I'm not good at facing people. If they have counterarguments, I try to find reasons why these counterarguments are good. I tend to interpret them favorably, whereas good debaters like my nephew, Arne, Jr., stick to their own arguments and fight every weak thing the opponent says — whereas I say, "Well, this is weak, that is not interesting to fight about."

DR: Is that really analytical training at work, or is it something else?

AN: Well, we need a minority among the fighters in the deep ecology movement who use their analytical upbringing. So I have something to offer. But there must not be too many in this special business. I am glad to say I feel that I am more interested in this social movement I call the deep ecology movement than I am in my own theorizing.

DR: So you're much more a figure in the movement than you are a philosopher of ecology?

AN: That's how I see myself. The philosophical contribution is to go behind the utility terminology of politics and raise interest far above contemporary politicians. We can mobilize people to consider their lives as a whole, contemplating what they basically stand for. Here, you go behind the scientific, ecological point of view. Scientifically, acid rain is very interesting and wonderful because of the fascinating changes it brings. In 1940, there were over two hundred insects here I could have noted, and now there are very few. A pure scientist would delight in these changes — so many new kinds of acid to explore!

But I speak of ecosophy: ecology blended with philosophy, wisdom related to action about people on earth. Wisdom transcends any science today or in the future. With ecosophy, politicians or decision makers will no longer push for more science, as much as they will push for more wisdom. Because however much more we get of science, ignorance will increase if we do not know the consequences of what we do by means of the science.

DR: And science can't give us those consequences?

AN: No.

DR: How can philosophers give them to us?

AN: The philosophers will not give you answers about the one thousand more chemicals now at large in our atmosphere. But the philosophers will, in a Socratic way, ask, "What will remain of goals in life?" There, they will find, I think, that the goals well understood by people are pleasure, happiness, and achievement. There is no requirement of tremendous population, tremendous buildings, or tremendous consumerism in order to have maximum pleasure, happiness, or achievement.

DR: So if you teach people how to articulate their goals in life, they will find that they're much more in line with the rest of natural creatures and plants and animals?

AN: Yes. And the philosophers are well trained to articulate these goals and the relations between goals and concrete situations. I talk about total views rather than philosophies. Views about who you are, your deepest wishes, your obligations, and your relations to others.

DR: So it's a matter once again of asking the right questions?

AN: Yes. Getting deeper. And in getting deeper, it seems to me, tremendous simplicity will come. You see, wisdom and simplicity go together.

DR: So what's a deep ecological philosophy? Just a set of questions?

AN: A deep ecological philosophy—I call that ecosophy—will offer answers to rather basic questions inspired, in part, by the ecological crisis, and these answers will differ tremendously for each seeker. But they have certain features in common, even on the rather general and abstract levels, and there I have the proposed eight points, which I stick to, though I make modifications every year.

DR: But those are points, I believe, for the movement, not the philosophy. That's a platform for the deep ecological movement, it seems to me—very different from philosophy.

AN: Well, those working together on any goal of global dimension should have certain general principles in common. But these principles should not imperil deep differences in ultimate metaphysical or religious views. Most deep ecologists have fundamental differences from each other, and speak in a variety of terminologies. Questioning one's motives leads inevitably to philosophical positions and from there back to practice.

DR: And any series of questions of purpose brings one quickly into philosophy.

AN: There, you see that you can affect people who are not used to asking such questions, who might say, "Oh well, of course I agree with your ideas, but politically I am a realist, I am fond of results. And given the framework that politicians give us, we are stuck. Of course, if this framework were changed, some of these changes I would very much like. And I might even make some profit within this new, stricter framework." So that very often they want to agree, and we will say, "Aha, now you have said it. Now we go together and try to make the politicians take the ecological crisis seriously . . ."

Example 1: More Power?

DR: Can you give me an example of a series of questions that leads from some practical considerations back to philosophy? Or I'll give you one, and you tell me how philosophy might help: Somebody wants to build a new hydropower plant . . .

AN: Yes. And they say, "We expect the need for electricity will increase, and as decision makers, we will be criticized heavily, because there is a shortage of electricity, and people might start using coal, for instance. So the new dam must be built." And then you say, "But are you sure there is a need for more electricity?" And they say, "Oh, yes, look at the chart here. There is this percentage increase." But you say, "There's a demand on a market—you call that a need?" And then, after some discussion, he replies, "No, no, no, of course not." There are a lot of demands that are not reflecting needs. "And so why do you think the increase in electricity demand will satisfy a need? If you are a person, you cannot submit yourself to demands unquestioningly. If other nations used as much electricity per person as in Norway, certainly there would be a catastrophe. We use even more per capita than in the United States. What's the ethical justification? Isn't it ethically necessary to level off energy use in Norway?"

It is my experience that this eager servant of the people, who would say "Yes!" to a hydroelectric plant, will accept practically everything you say as a philosopher. And what they will do is say, "That's too early, it's not yet politically possible. Politics is the art of the possible. Do you want me to leave politics?" — or something like that. To which you should say, "I see your point, yes. I see your point. We have a distant goal formulated on the basis of much deeper premises than you have in your argumentation. All we can ask of you is, at least once a year, to admit that you agree with us. Take the long-range view!" If this politician from then on, from time to time, formulates some of these basic long-term goals, then his argumentation pattern is not shallow, and he is saved, so to speak.

Example 2: Eskimos and Whales

DR: Well, do you think the Eskimos should still be killing seals and whales?

AN: Not those that are nearly extinct, and never when they use only part of the whale, and then sell it in a way that resembles the practice in rich nations. Then they must be stopped. But as long as it belongs to the culture, of course they can kill whales, even if there are very few.

DR: But we have a problem with this, because other cultures, such as the Norwegian whaling industry, have, you know, gotten rid of most of the whales, so the Eskimos really can't live the way they did before without damaging the world's population of a rare species. Now how do you deal with this? It seems to be something of an ethical dilemma.

AN: Well, yes. I think the trouble is that we have killed so many that there are only a few left, and then we say to the Eskimos, "You cannot have more." I do think that if there's a genuine culture, they should kill all they can, for their own use. The Norwegian whalers, now without work, could be hired as inspectors to see that none but Eskimos kill whales.

DR: Your answer makes the problem too simple. Because there are so few of these species left, it is simply impossible to let the Eskimos kill them in the manner they are used to. They simply can't do it and sustain the practice in today's depleted world.

AN: Oh, yes, they can. What they can't do is to take up our methods of using the whale.

DR: Assume that we've decimated the population so much that, at present, it is ecologically unsound for these people to continue the practices that used to be sustainable. Assume there are fifteen left in the world, and we can't let them kill even one. Assume that this is the case. What do you tell them?

AN: Oh, then, of course I would offer any kind of meat for them, in any kind of volume, in order to say, "Don't kill any whales for the next ten years."

DR: . . . knowing that this would destroy their culture? Knowing that it would affect them in such a way that it would be hard for them to get back to the old ways? How would you deal with this conflict?

It's a bit unrealistic, because we know that Eskimos have had so much contact with the outside world, and with alcoholism and with the modern world so nearby, it's pretty much of an imaginary example. It's not a pristine culture, this one. But is any culture truly pristine in this time in which we have all become so aware of each other around the world? The issue I'm trying to bring up is: Are there some times when a pristine culture needs to sacrifice its ways for the world ecological situation? How do you deal with this kind of ethical conflict?

AN: We'll probably have a lot of such conflicts in the next century. At the moment, the situation is unclear. Yet, I would give the culture a priority. A whole human culture has the priority over extinction of one or several animal species—but only if the cultural difference is deep enough from all others.

DR: Now, what about the fact that these cultures will inevitably come into contact with those things that we find distasteful about the modern world. They're going to come across our civilization. How do we prepare them to be strong when they learn about America and want to be like America? Just like Eastern Europe, just like people in India, and everywhere.

AN: Well, it's not very different from what we see in Norway, except the Samé people in arctic Norway possess this feeling of being proud of nature, that to have such nature as habitat is, from the European point of view, unique, and we should do all we can to prevent building a factory here instead of some more sustainable activity. Listen to those who have a proposal for a way of life that is sustainable in the high Arctic, where the pride and joy of the place is important, along with their local willingness to have a policy of coastal fisheries, and other things that immediately meet the requirements of the reindeer-herding Samé people—yes, yes, yes—so that you give them the maximum opportunity to continue. It is the Samé people who must wish deeply to continue their way of life, and what is tragic is that thousands of them prefer to continue their culture without external decimation.

And a rich state like Norway has the economic power to have a policy that would allow those people who like the traditional cultural pattern of the Arctic to continue. Let those who want go south into factories, but let those people themselves have the chance to choose.

Human or Natural?

DR: There are many people who use your term "deep ecology" to mean a concern for nature that goes on apart from concern for people.

AN: I deplore this. There need never be such opposition. In Africa, the World Wildlife Fund once suggested that certain tribespeople take only one egg from the nest of a certain bird, instead of taking all eggs in the neighborhood. When no more of that kind of bird is in the neighborhood, they go farther away, taking all eggs from the more distant place, and so on. And then the bird simply gets extinct. So those who have an affinity with deep ecology, they say, "Take only one egg from each nest, because you need that, it's a vital need." And they will still get this tremendous joy from the birds, and they will not go extinct. Birds and humans coexist easily.

DR: What about people who say, "Earth first!"—exclamation point—and want to set aside large areas of wilderness from which people, or at least the wrong kind of people, are excluded?

AN: "Earth First!" is a splendid slogan in the United States. But there is a tendency in the deep ecology movement to say, "Earth first!" in the sense that we are more fond of nature than of people. Priorities should always have an ecological base before thinking only of their human value. Historically, it is interesting that from boyhood, I heard people engaged in conservation or very eager for conservation of nature praising the people living in the mountains. I had some friends among the small, tiny farms where the sheep are high up in the mountains. They were proud of that. When I was fourteen years old, when I first got in the real mountains of Norway, in Jotunheimen, I met people who lived there year round. I liked that very much, of course, and I would wish to stay there all winter long. What a tragedy when people who belong out in free nature had to become citizens, city people, because of some kind of economic changes. I think in the deep ecology movement also, you will find people who are so much in love with this free, distant, but human, kind of life, but are not in love with people who destroy it.

DR: But I believe there are two different ways of arguing here: One of them is to say, you have to care about these open, free, wild areas of nature, because when you care about them, and when you set them aside, it enlarges who you are as a person; it increases your Self-realization, because you're identifying with a larger Self, while still retaining your narrow ego-self. There's another view that says you're doing that because the earth is more important than people, and we have to recognize our place and set aside some things that are beyond our influence. And I think these are two distinct and different approaches.

AN: I don't see them as being incompatible. In the deep ecology movement, this kind of empathy for other living beings is a very deep-seated premise. I think we all agree that a father who has no options but to kill the last animal of this or that species, or to ruin the last patch of tropical forest, in order to feed a baby that otherwise will be ruined through hunger, just has to kill or burn. There's no question of that. But Americans and Norwegians are ruining what's left of our free nature without good reason, and that's a crime.

DR: You're still not answering my question. Why is it a crime? Is it because we shouldn't think only of ourselves? Or is it because if we understood ourselves better, we would protect these things because they're part of us also?

AN: If you use the term, "to do something for its own sake," then you will do it for the sake of the free nature.

DR: But the argument from Self-realization as a norm suggests something else—it suggests that you're doing it for yourself.

AN: Yes, like Gandhi would say. When he was asked, "How do you do these altruistic things all year long?" he said, "I am not doing something altruistic at all. I am trying to improve in Self-realization."

DR: Yes, sure, but do you see the difference and the importance of making it clear? Because there's a strong movement that wants to separate these two things. And you want to connect them in a way that's different, I think, from the stewardship ideal.

AN: Oh, certainly.

DR: But that's also saying, "Take care of the world because it's here for us." That's not so different from, "Take care of the world, it makes us who we are."

AN: The "us" there presupposes that the human ego is something that cannot be enlarged and deepened. Only people who are very narrow in their perspective and feelings make this tremendous cleavage between the self and the surrounding of the self. Aristotle, you know, talked about the social self: There are no egos that are nonsocial—society is there from the very beginning of one's development. Here, in the ecological movement, you see the ecological self, and you do not accept this cleavage.

So is it for humans, or is it for free nature? You must specify whether it's a father with hungry children, looking for the last things that can be eaten, and so on. And there, you, of course, have a very narrow utilitarian experience of reality. This narrow utilitarian experience of reality makes for the cleavage. I say narrow utilitarianism because, as Spinoza would say, the most useful things you have are your friends. But he didn't mean that you shouldn't acknowledge the separate intrinsic value of these people. Why should something intrinsically valuable not also be useful?

DR: It seems there is a basic premise in ecological thinking that nature has the answers; people are looking to something out there called nature, saying this is where we find out what's right. It goes back to Aristotle. It comes up very often, and very rarely do you read things that go beyond it. If we paid attention to nature, we would know how to live correctly.

AN: If we paid attention? Already this cleavage is very strange. Nature is supposed to know best, in the sense that we can learn everything from nature?

DR: I run across many budding ecologists who believe that nature has the answers, if we would just pay attention. Often, little more is said. I'm pointing this out as a kind of general tendency that rarely looks beyond the initial level. Some say, "If we built houses so that they were in a natural style and fit in with the landscape, that would be better than building a highway straight across the river. Or if we built small-scale hydroplants that took just enough energy . . ."

AN: But mountains are tremendously big. Some of nature wants to make big things. Why not compare, then, buildings with mountains?

DR: Well, such people rarely say, go ahead and build a building as big as a mountain.

AN: You should let nature teach you, and look at this big, big mountain. We could make a big, big house.

DR: Right, but usually that's not said, because people are looking for a certain kind of idea in nature, and they imagine it is there and claim it as their authority.

AN: Well, I think there is something in what you are saying, but I think you underestimate people who are concerned with ecology.

DR: Well, I'm just trying to point out that maybe there's a philosophical difficulty in asking for so much from nature, in this way that a lot of people like to do.

AN: I have the feeling, from when you have a long talk with someone who would like to live ecologically, that they don't often make such shortcuts like that.

DR: But I do find, in the time that I've spent a lot of time talking to you over the years, many areas where you seem to refuse to go deeper, and refuse to consider possible differences or complexities in the situation. I wonder if that's true—or maybe it's just me.

AN: Hmm. More than an incapacity to go deeper, I may have a resistance against going deeper. And, of course, I enjoy it when you or others try to make me go deeper where I avoid it. I cannot admit that I have the weakness, and I will be glad when I overcome such an obstacle, going further. If I have to change my views on a very basic point? Important, difficult, but ultimately painful . . .

DR: I think it's more of a change in the articulation of certain points. Perhaps you should rely less on slogans, and more on some kind of message and instructions that people should not just take your words at face value and repeat them back, but somehow go beyond.

AN: But I thought I was one of those who make it extremely difficult to have disciples, because the moment somebody says something that looks like what I have said, I immediately try to make them uncomfortable, changing formulations to improve them?

DR: Yes, it's true. But less so now . . . It seems with the whole movement into ecosophy and deep ecology, you want everybody to join up without trying to discuss too much about what it means, except that these people really care, so they must be on the right track.

AN: Yes, I have made a lot of fuss about this, as I feel there are hundreds of thousands of people who really belong to the deep ecology movement but don't know it.

DR: Well, a lot of people don't want to be included in it, because they think of it as an extreme point of view that tends to put nature before people. Yet, it doesn't seem to me that that's really what you're saying.

AN: Oh, no.

DR: Perhaps you haven't made it clear enough.

AN: That's right. There's a norm I could formulate like this: You and your group and your institutions and your nation cannot behave in a way you consider desirable for everybody, if you know that everybody cannot have that kind of life. It's a Kantian kind of thing.

Social versus Deep

DR: What do you think the real difference is between social and deep ecology?

AN: Well, in South America, more than fifty percent of one's work as an ecologist will be to live with poor people, instructing them and getting instruction from them, and learning old tribal ecological insights. So concern for poverty and needs is in their minds much more of the time than those in rich nations trying to counteract destruction of old-growth forests.

The elite of the poor world take their signals very much from the United States, and when they see that the United States (and

Norway, of course!) has practically no concern for these woods, they say, "Why should we do anything?" It's a crime, because we destroy our credibility as advisers. The elite in a poor country know that we destroy much more per capita than they do. In Calcutta, they destroy very little per capita. I don't think that Ehrlich and others who have talked about setting aside wilderness areas have concrete plans in the Third World. Within the deep ecology movement, we must be very careful, and say, "I am now talking about the United States, I am talking about a rich country. I am not talking about Tanzania; the millions of people who live sustainably in tropical areas are of tremendous value, because they have deeply different cultures, and they know how to continue to live their own ways. But now there are too many people to sustain the old ways." So what can be done? Well, we must get away from the notion that subsistence agriculture is any kind of solution to the problem of overpopulation. There will be more and more urbanized people, and that means that we must have sustainable economic relations to these urbanized people through the exchange of goods.

In Norway, I know that it's very difficult, because Norwegians say, "We have to buy from Germany, because we wish to export to Germany. And therefore we will not import certain things from the Third World, because they are not important trading partners for us. And we can stop exporting to Kenya; that makes no difference to Norwegian national productivity." There are terrific ethical problems here.

DR: But the deep ecology movement is never going to be about everything. It's not good to claim to solve all problems. People who are attracted to it are those who care about preserving nature, for whatever reason. Either they like to go outside and walk in the wilderness, or maybe they're scientists and recognize the grave danger we're in. It's not a movement that's going to attract everyone. It's not really about saving the world. It's about a limited thing, and I think that's important to realize. It's not really concerned with development problems. Its primary aim is preserving nature for those who perceive that nature is important.

AN: Free nature for meditation and contemplation.

DR: Yes, but preserving it especially for those who appreciate it.

AN: No, no. True, the deep ecology movement has a modest niche in the world, and it is useless to pretend that it comprises too much. You ask many specific questions, and it must be understood that to be a supporter of the deep ecology movement does not require answers similar to mine. Very few supporters of the deep ecology movement know my terminology or my writings. I have merely pointed out a movement that I insist is already there, long before I gave it a name.

DR: That's possible. But I think the movement should just stop and say, "These are some things we're not going to talk about, because we're not interested in them." Rather than trying to have a superficial view on what trade should be, what development should be. Either that or they need to learn a lot more about other things. They need to look at a Third World country and see more than rare species of animals.

AN: But I completely agree! Therefore, it's very important to be aware of at least three tremendous movements today. We have the Green movement, we have the social justice movement, we have the peace movement. And within the Green movement, you have the deep ecology movement. I hope people in the social justice movement, concerned with poverty and all these things, will tolerate much of the deep ecology movement, without propagating the tenets of deep ecology at all. They will talk very much about the limitations. And there I will say, "Oh, certainly it's limited." And the peace movement will never be part of the deep ecology movement. There have been many, many wars since the deep ecology movement started. And there is nothing more devastating to the ecology than a war. These movements will never merge into one, but their interests do overlap.

Within the ecology movement there is a lot of mutual complaint: People are described in caricatures, with very few sentences—whereas in real life, more or less responsible people have very complex ways of being, beyond the limits of any rule or stereotype.

DR: But moralizing is a big part of the deep ecology movement. People say, "I am deep and you are shallow."

AN: No, that's not at all moralizing. It just seems that according to my hypothesis, only deep changes or a significant change in society in the future would be enough to have any effect on our state of decay. The shallow argumentation says, "That's not necessary. You need not go deep in this direction."

DR: I think that's more of a reduction of reality, which is that some people are working on specific problems and simply don't have time to worry about the deep changes that are not immediate. And they work on concrete solutions. They build a cleaner car, rather than lobbying for why we should take the bus. I am afraid that some people invoke the name of deep ecology to say that these people are shallow.

AN: Oh, that is very unfortunate, because that's never been my intention behind this terminology. If somebody is working on less-polluting cars, that may be a part of a total view.

The Infinity of Ecologies

DR: Is deep ecology one-sided? When the message is more for people who just love nature and they feel this empathy with the natural world, there's a danger that they begin to loathe urban life and shun it, and I think that's the wrong direction for the future. People need to recognize the connection between urban life and the love of the natural world.

AN: Do you wish to contribute to the solution to the ecological crisis? To fight for wide sustainability is more than just evading catastrophes. It's to demand richness and diversity of life! Including habitats. Including a diversity of ways of attacking the problem. Never demand that everyone share your values.

It reminds me of Otto Neurath, the logical empiricist. He had this tendency to classify every philosopher or logician he liked as friends of logical empiricism, which was his particular philosophy. They laughed. First of all, they were not interested in his problems. Second, if they were, he probably wouldn't like them.

DR: It's the same with the deep ecologists.

AN: Yes. I often say, "But you are really a supporter of deep ecology. You just don't know it." Some think that deep ecology should encompass questions of peace and social justice, whereas I think we should be careful to distinguish the differences between these movements, and not spread oneself too thin. But what, then, distinguishes me from some of these others is that I am so eager to admit immediately that I am one-sided in this way and that I see that there are infinitely many other possible interpretations of the world.

DR: But you're not usually so ready to admit that maybe something like deep ecology is one-sided.

AN: No. Honesty is not one-sided. You couldn't say that history is one-sided because it doesn't take into account mathematics.

DR: But the difference is that history is a wide form of study. Deep ecology is one kind of ideology of looking at the world that emphasizes the importance of free and wild nature. And one can easily look at it and realize that, when it comes to talking about things that don't have much to do with wild nature, it's kind of empty and not complete. It doesn't yet have much to say about culture or society or cities, just a few derogatory generalizations.

AN: But, you see, if I talk to someone who is dealing with questions of urbanization, then I am very eager to say that this has helped tremendously with things I do and it's certainly compatible with being a supporter of the deep ecology movement.

DR: But do you have anything to offer people working on these specific problems? It's almost like a kind of Communist platform to say, "Join us because we support you," without really giving so much, because the orientation of deep ecology is so much in one direction—as we've talked about probably enough.

AN: You mean the theoreticians of the movement?

DR: Yes, and the people in it are doing it because they want to save something in the distance, something apart from humanity, and there's no reason that they need to say much about the urban problems, unless they claim to be more than they are. If you just say, "This is a movement for wilderness preservation," fine. If it's a whole social movement, if it's a whole new way of life, then it really needs to deepen itself before even having the name. It only gets to be a problem if either theoreticians or the supporters act or claim as if they have a more comprehensive view than they, in fact, have. If someone admits "I've got an approach to wilderness preservation called 'deep ecology,' " that's one thing. To say it's a whole new way to look at human habitation on the earth is something else, and I think it's an issue of vagueness again.

AN: Yes, but most European ecopolitical thinkers don't know about wilderness practically, because there it's a question of free nature and not wilderness, and free nature may be a small patch of fairly undisturbed nature where small children can play. This is basic. Then people ask, "Well, how do you define it?" And I say that social movements are not easily defined — conservatism, liberalism, the peace movement — the definitions are so uninteresting, because you have one sentence or two sentences. It's so arbitrary what you say. So I will not define what it means to go deep!

Theoreticians of the deep ecology movement should be very careful not to exploit their own favorite way of life, to say, "Look at me, I'm in the wilderness, or I'm in a cottage high up in the mountains like Tvergastein, and look how I am living," as if it would be a good idea to have more people in Holland or Belgium, for instance, getting out of their homelands and into the mountains. As citizens of these nations, they have other more pressing issues. I agree with you that some of us have not been careful enough, because Naess is also a mountaineer and he has a hut that's very well known because it's so high and exposed. That's all bad, but what's good is that in the ten or more years I have spent up here I have enjoyed an extremely low standard of living. I am so sure that if we in the rich world could decrease our standard of living and I was not supposed to get out of the country more than once in ten years and then for a very definite purpose, then I would gladly say, "Yes, that's fine for me." And that holds for other theoreticians of deep ecology, I suppose. They will be glad to cut out practically all comfort in life.

It might be better if they had done so in cities, living in the slums. And there Gandhi is a fine example, because he had real association with wild nature and small animals and big animals and all these things. He was doing his job in the slums and would insist on living there, caring for all creatures.

DR: You can be all for the preservation of nature and the protection of it and still live and work in the city.

AN: Exactly. The frontier is long, and what I am saying is that whatever you advocate, long-range ecological sustainability should be one requirement.

DR: Now is that word "sustainability" a powerful word because it's vague? Why do you use it?

AN: What are the necessary conditions of sustainability? To give a set of sufficient conditions ought to be important for the clarification of this idea. There should be large-scale research going on, all over the world, focusing on terms like this that are in vogue, that everybody is suddenly trying to use, creating confusion first of all.

DR: Except it's the ambiguity that leads the terms to communicate to people, like the slogans that have attracted so many to deep ecology. It is somewhat similar to the appeal of the term "democracy," which you so examined in the early fifties.

AN: Yes. That's one of the important things to clarify: how these certain ambiguities have positive functions, and how they have negative functions.

DR: If you really believe that terms should be defined and stated and specifically introduced, how come you never do it in your own writings, which are generally riddled with vague statements in various directions that are not so clear and not so unambiguous and lead to all kinds of conflicting interpretations? It's not clarity that you're presenting!

AN: It is fascinating to hear you speak like that. In the early 1970s I wrote with a high level of precision and clarity, for example, on the uses of the term "nature." Are we a part of it, or apart from it? Many conflicting paths of reasoning there. But what I wrote and talked about then made little difference. I couldn't manage to keep it up, because nobody seemed to care. They responded much better to vague, embracing slogans. But after hearing you now, I start to wonder what would have happened if I and others had continued to write more precisely — would more people today be taking our questions seriously and systematically? I do not know.

On the other hand, some of the ambiguity in my writings on deep ecology is due in part to the real difficulty of articulating basic intuitions about the universe. People are frustrated that I can base an entire book on intuitions that are nowhere defined or explained. It is tantalizing for our culture, this seeming lack of explanation. But if you hear a phrase like, "All life is fundamentally one," you should be open to *tasting* this, before asking immediately, "What does this mean?" There is a kind of deep *yes* to nature that is central to my philosophy. What do we say yes to? Very difficult to find out — there is a deep unconditionality, but at the same time a kind of regret, sorrow, or displeasure. Nature is not brutal, but we do see brutality. As we see yellow in the sun. As we see these fantastic gray clouds outside this window . . .

VIII: SEEING THE WORLD ANEW

*I*n the preceding chapter, deep ecology was described as a way
of grounding environmental concern in basic philosophical
questions, or a long search for the roots of our ills in the dark
caverns of ideas behind the whole movement of civilization. But
for Arne Naess, there is a whole other side to deep ecology that
has to do with a renovation of the way we see the world, asking
for a new kind of perception that looks for interconnected
wholes, of which we are always a part. When we glimpse a
mountain, a tree, or a factory, we need to learn to see not only
objects but patterns whose origin and purpose are deeply
entwined with our own. These patterns that appear as wholes are
called gestalts, the German word for "shapes," a usage loosely
derived from the gestalt psychologists of the early part of this
century. These men — Wolfgang Köhler, Kurt Lewin, and others —
investigated the way we perceive ourselves as fitting into larger
patterns that contain us as a sign of mental balance. As Arne sees
it, these gestalts are not mere psychological devices that allow
human minds to make sense of things. They are instead the com-
ponents of an ontology, the technical term for "the way things
are."

The reason to think of the world in this way is to derive a
vision in which humanity is not opposed to nature, in which we
are no longer subjects with the world our object. With proper
training in this mode of thought, it should become impossible to
oppose our interests to the world's, and the nature that includes

humanity will look like a whole different place, where our eco-
logical mistakes and successes will be far more clear.

How can we make this vision more precise? Once more, I try
to get Arne to clarify his terms; once more, he leads me astray
from one topic to another to another. Again we have an appeal-
ing vision that pulls us along without limiting itself. Vagueness
prevails where precision does not. Or am I, too, pulled into a
pattern that cannot be fully described, because I am snared
within it, along with everyone else . . . ?

Gestalts Undefined

DR: You often say that you're not so much concerned with environmental ethics—how we should behave in regard to nature—as
you are interested in describing the world in a new way. You
often use the word "gestalt" to suggest the new way. What do
you mean?

AN: In order to have more people engaged actively and joyfully
in the ecological movement, one should not talk about duties
very often, because it is clear from the history of humankind that
duties do not play a great role for most people most times,
whereas what people like to do and what they like to think have
played tremendous roles. And what we like to do and like to
think depend on how we conceive the world, how we conceive
facts, and what kind of facts we would like to contemplate and
consider. That is to say, how reality is rather than what you
ought to do and what you ought to think. Mostly we act according to how we see reality. So, therefore, I go into ontology: doc-
trines about the way things are.

When I travel by train through the woods, I see the branches
being joyful or depressed, the trees as old or young, some of
them even dancing. Rushing forward, or falling down, even when
they remain on the tree. I believe these qualities to be in the tree,
not just in my experience of the tree.

Gestalt psychology imagines that the patterns of people's
experiences are something going on in their heads. It imagines
that people have images of the tree in their minds, but why stop
there? Get rid of the subject as a container of images and

thoughts. It's all just as much out there as it is in you! You can only make this partition between object, subject, and medium through logical analysis, whereas spontaneous life is without clear divisions. The gestalt ontology is in the world.

DR: So you agree with philosophers like William James and John Dewey, who say that experience is primary. Not in the head, not in the world, but just the human experience, first before minds or worlds are imagined?

AN: Well, if you add the term "human," then it's lost again. Reality has nothing in particular to do with humans.

DR: But what other experience do we know about?

AN: Of course we can only talk about human experience, but I'm talking about the content of reality. I'm sure that other living beings have also experienced reality.

DR: How about dead beings? How about rocks?

AN: I don't think they have experienced reality.

DR: So it's a life-centered theory of experience?

AN: Yes. I don't know how far down the so-called kingdom of animals you can go. The essential thing is that we must avoid the thought of things in themselves that Kant talked about as *Ding an Sich*, a reality apart from the sensed world.

DR: He thought that was inaccessible to us.

AN: Absolutely, he thought even the law of causality is imposed by the subject, us.

DR: Right. Are you, then, closer to Martin Heidegger, in his investigation of human *Dasein*, being-in-the-world?

AN: He's trying! But Heidegger needs to have a strange terminology to move in the direction of this gestalt ontology. Of course it's very ambiguous, very difficult to get a straight concept out of him. Phenomenology has this concept of lifeworld—that is to say, you try to describe spontaneous experience without having any kind of notion whether it is real or not real, or whether there is a rainbow [a rainbow appears outside our window across the Hardangervidda] or not. The rainbow is a very good example of a thing that gestalt ontology will take care of very well. It does not exist without the perceiver noticing it, looking up at the sky at the right place and time, in the ambiguity between sun and cloud. Today we cannot clearly distinguish mathematics from physics anymore, and you reach the position of a philosopher like Eino Kaila, who has insisted all the time that science would never get at any knowledge except structure. And I am not after abstract structure, and in modern quantum physics and general relativity, that is what they go for.

DR: Those are not experience structures.

AN: No. Impossible. But they are extremely important abstract structures. The abstraction within mathematical physics is at a much higher level today than in 1913, the time of the atomic view of nature. Now it is getting overwhelmingly clear that the terms "waves" and "particles" have nothing in common with anything in the neighborhood of our spontaneous experience of reality. The scientific image is a view of abstract structures that does not touch spontaneous experience. And that is why we need a kind of gestalt ontology—how can we cling to particles or waves to explain our experience?

DR: Are there always competing gestalts of ways of looking at things?

AN: Oh, yes. But they are not competing in the sense of conflict between the emanation of reality that is going on in Bergsonian time, *durée*—that is, something enduring and lived, which is not at all a concept in physics. They use the term "time," but it is defined in terms of space. It's not duration.

DR: But you look for evidence in experience, right? I don't think you're presenting a theory.

AN: Yes. It's an ontological theory. About abstract structures of relativity in relation to concrete reality. And concrete reality will have this gestalt character, that is to say, no part and no wholes but subordinate and superordinate gestalts.

DR: But what if the interpretations disagree? Is there only one right way of looking at a piece of reality?

AN: Well, this is ontology, and it belongs to the level of ultimate views of ultimate philosophic conceptions. These are rarely comparable. So it's not possible to think that there would be only one . . .

DR: So there is no single right reality accessible through this gestalt method. What if someone disagrees with you, and doesn't feel at home with your particular gestalt vision of the laughing birch tree?

AN: That would be very interesting for me.

DR: Well, who has the correct vision of the gestalt? How does this gestalt approach differ from subject/object perceptions? You could take the landscape and the weather here at Tvergastein and someone could say, "It's beautiful, I love it here," and someone else might say, "It's cold, it's terrible, it's raining all the time." I mean, who is right?

Imagine We Are under a Waterfall

AN: No, no. Imagine that we are now underneath Niagara Falls or the Vøringfoss.

DR: All right.

AN: And one person experiences this reality as a big water factory gone awry, something dangerous. The danger and anxiety will be part of the gestalt at that moment. This is one content of reality that I cannot get into touch with.

DR: This particular interpretation?

AN: Well, it's not an interpretation. It's someone else's spontaneous experience of reality that is not accessible to me. And I am glad I have my own experience of this Vøringfoss or Niagara as something entirely delightful.

DR: So all of these possible experiences of reality are part of reality?

AN: Yes.

DR: Even by people who haven't been born yet, or who've died? Right now, all possible experiences of this view are part of that view, and no one will ever know all of the different ones or be able to apprehend all of them, because there are so many differences. What is this telling us, exactly? What's the point?

AN: The point is that you get rid of many difficulties you have in conceiving yourself as having inner experiences that are subjective and cannot be taken seriously in politics. I refer now to ecological debates, when certain things are discounted because they are considered subjective, and we are told to consider only facts, leaving out what is "personal."

DR: Right. So you're just announcing that all experiences are part of the world and should be taken seriously.

AN: That's not enough to announce. I would like to help people who say, "For me, this waterfall is dangerous and just a mess of wasted hydropower." They have a negative experience of reality. I can coax people into joyful experiences, and they will learn that these are just as real as the cost/benefit analyses commissioned by the state.

DR: But why is that kind of open relativism going to help in any ecological conflict? Someone could just say, "Wait a minute, I think this place is terrible. It needs to be dammed up and turned into a multilevel amusement park." You know, listen to my experience. You're opening many cans of worms here.

AN: But that's not experience. Those people would like us to only think that abstract structures are reality.

DR: Why are you assuming that?

AN: Because, you see, they speak about facts . . .

DR: Those were not facts I was speaking about. I was speaking about experience. You're saying you enjoy this place and you feel it's a part of yourself, and I'm giving you my plan for enriching an experience that at present seems unfulfilled.

AN: I see what you mean.

DR: All you're doing is opening up a more free-ranging discussion. You know, subjectivism on both sides. I don't quite see what the advantage would be.

AN: Well, the difference is that the people who are used to living in completely humanly determined environments like cities tend to look upon everything else as some kind of material part of reality that can be used in their way of life. They use abstract conceptions of usefulness that imply that the more people have their kind of experience, the fewer possibilities there are to save the wild and free, because they will say, "Out there, it's ugly."

DR: Why should saving things have anything to do with this kind of view? You're not talking about any duties or rights . . .

AN: Because the potentials for experiences with simple means are so much greater if you have a very well educated view of gestalts. Whereas if you see the whole outside world as a tool—here, this can be used for digging coal, here can be used for electricity— you have a very primitive way of seeing, which makes it extremely difficult to get people motivated toward sustainability.

For instance, we try, in prison, to get criminals to view other people in different ways. But they have gestalts in which very many things are threatening. In psychiatry, you have specialists who are able to treat psychotic patients who certainly see the doctor as a combined gestalt of their mother or father in terrible conflict. They are ultimately able to say, "I see my father in your arms there," and they can then describe what they see.

What we must try to do is to make the patient see other parts of reality which make it possible for them to live by themselves and not in institutions that cost millions of dollars. And the same with the technocrats bent on eradicating free nature. We should treat them like these psychiatry patients!

DR: This gestalt approach of yours seems to be a kind of analytical tool for reorganizing society, by getting people to see certain kinds of gestalts that you think are better than others. There is a certain morality here. You are interested in ethics!

Does Arne Naess Believe in Right and Wrong?

AN: No, but I do have goals.

DR: You are picking some ways of looking at reality and saying, "These are better, for some reason." You do return to a kind of environmental ethics in the end. Only it's an ethics of gestalts.

AN: I don't know if this is ethics. It's an ontology . . .

DR: It's a judgment between ontologies.

AN: . . . as an instrument, to approach wider sustainability.

DR: OK. And that's some sort of norm you're using: sustainability!

AN: Well, it would be a great thing to achieve ecological sustainability.

Beethoven

DR: I think you ought to try defining what you mean by gestalt for this discussion.

AN: Well, definitions are very difficult for me, as you know.

DR: They don't have to be exact, but just so people know what we're talking about, because it's not entirely clear to me, and it won't be clear to them. Your "gestalt" is something like a pattern that holds together as a whole, that makes a kind of unified sense, more than just the parts of experience. It is like this, but is it more?

AN: In gestalt psychology, they say that the whole is more than the sum of the parts. But this can be misleading. I can use a symphony as an example. In Beethoven's Fifth Symphony, you have "da da da DAH." And that is already forming music, a kind of gestalt. And then you have the next phrase. It appears the same, but not "da da da DAH," it is instead "da da da DAW." That's the next whole. And when you get to this second gestalt, it cannot be fully experienced without the first one. Because it is part of the symphony. And you go on to themes and developments and movements and then the symphony as a whole. There are subordinate and superordinate gestalts in, say, ten or twenty layers, and the whole is more than the parts, but also the parts are more than the whole, because there's nothing left if you just have the whole. You have to continue, like in the nature mysticism of Spinoza, to keep the most subordinate gestalt you have. You keep them all. You cannot say, "Now I am free of the particulars."

A larger, still more encompassing gestalt is the spontaneous experience of a definite occasion where the Fifth Symphony is played. And then you get into it, consider how you are connected to the people in the orchestra, and what you experienced yesterday and what you have experienced just before the concert. All this then determines a total experience that is not real as a totality but where all the subordinate gestalts of these different kinds come together in a unity, in one experience.

DR: What about those aspects of the symphony that cannot come clear in a sudden experience? First of all, it is an experience through time, not an instant, and second, there's the fact that you need to study it quite a lot to understand all the relationships that are there. You don't just feel them in a moment.

AN: Yes, yes. And when you are extremely young the first time you hear it, well then, it is something else. Completely different. Even people who are much in love with just this kind of music don't always have the ability to compare what they experience of reality to that of all others. But the Fifth Symphony is an abstract structure. It is not a content of reality.

DR: Right. However you look at it, it's still an abstract structure. Well, OK, how would you use this to talk about some kind of problem in the world, some sort of environmental quandary, since that is your stated aim of this approach?

The Road through the Forest

AN: Well, let us consider a forest, and discuss plans for building a road through this forest. A technocrat might say the road through the forest is only one one-millionth part of this forest, and it doesn't matter at all to have that road. But then critics would say, "Well, it shouldn't go through the heart of the forest." And they say, "Heart of the forest, nonsense! Let's have facts here," and for facts, he points out the abstract structure of geography and he says, "This is the real forest, here." And for him the "real" forest is what I call an "abstract structure." And if most people are overwhelmed by these abstract structures, they say, "Let us have the road, because this talk about the heart of the forest, and of the different qualities you have in the forest if it is far from any road, that is just subjective, and those who feel them are a small minority."

DR: Well, what if he instead asks, "You people who are looking at the heart of the forests, what's your intention, what's the limit of your consideration? You're thinking of this as some abstract thing that you want to protect, with a heart and all this. Whereas I am thinking of all the people living on the two sides of the forest, how they use the forest, how they need to communicate with each other. I have a larger gestalt in mind, and your view is too limited, because it looks only at the heart of the forest for you."

AN: No. Some of the people living around the forest do not communicate only with themselves, but with the forest as well. They go into the woods, and therefore they have a richer part of reality within reach. The more people around who have this and can articulate what they have, and can point out that what this technocrat has in mind is destructive, the better.

DR: But what if that's not what they have in mind?

AN: Pardon me?

DR: What if the person you call a technocrat has in mind a larger gestalt that involves more people, and has decided that this is an embracing, more present gestalt that requires this road? It's not facts that motivate him, but a larger, more inclusive whole. How are you going to argue against that, using your gestalt approach?

AN: Only by seeing through his descriptions. His descriptions would probably be very primitive from a richness of gestalt point of view . . .

DR: Why must it be so?

AN: Why? Because all his education is to forget about spontaneous experience!

DR: You're not paying attention to my example. Forget the technical side. Just assume there's a person who thinks in a gestalt manner, but who happens to perceive the world in such a way that there's a larger, richer, more important gestalt that involves people who need to communicate through the forest by way of the road. He might say, "I have a vision here. It fits together these people and this forest. A road is just what they need, this is the way I see it." I'm explaining it to you, not only with facts. I'm explaining a gestalt picture. What I want to know is, why is the gestalt approach particularly friendly to the preservation of nature as opposed to the putting forth of any particular argument, if phrased in the right way? Are there certain natural gestalts that are more important than things people might want to connect in their whole views? I don't understand why your approach is necessarily one for the environmental movement.

AN: At least in this century, the education in planning at the universities teaches how to go against the gestalt ontology of spontaneous experience in favor of more data, more rationality. Because if they have all these gestalt experiences, why don't they speak about them in their reports and in the documents they deliver to the higher authorities? Why do they speak the way they do?

DR: It's another kind of gestalt they're working with. What you seem to be asking for is a very particular kind of gestalt that says, "My experience of this is what I should try to communicate to people." That's not gestalt ontology in itself. It's a certain kind. For all you know, these planners may experience what they're looking at in terms of these figures and facts they are trained to assess, and you can't say that's not a gestalt. Unless there is a particular kind of gestalt that you like better than others!

AN: But why do they hide them? They are hiding them.

DR: They're not hiding from gestalts in general. They're hiding a particular kind of gestalt, and you have yet to articulate what it is that you like.

AN: The language they use is what I don't like. It is a quantitative language, which does not go into particulars, such as the heart of the forest . . .

DR: Look at the *Samla* [Master] *Plan* in Norway. One of the criteria in the Samla Plan for Norwegian watershed development is to examine how beautiful a watershed is. They have these tests, and they quantify how beautiful it is. And this is one of the criteria they use to determine whether they should build a dam there. There's a bunch of others: whether it's good for wildlife, whether it has archaeological significance, what the recreational potential is—and they add all of these up and have a total view. Now, why isn't that a particular gestalt view of the watershed? It seems to me that this is one kind of gestalt, just as much a part of the material being examined. Unless you give me some criteria that say how direct experience is more fundamental than education in the formation of gestalt views. You haven't said anything about this yet.

AN: But do you think, then, that I am talking about beauty, for instance?

DR: No, I think you're talking about individual experience and not the content of the world. It's a very fuzzy vision, very imprecise. Dangerously so.

AN: Well, we couldn't go further without taking some of the forest documents and comparing them with our own experience. And, for instance, they might consider the beauty of a certain view from a certain point. But they will not ask about the beauty of the forest as a whole. They would probably propose a road so that more people can get to this beautiful place.

DR: You want to say there is some kind of naturally continuous gestalt sense of a place that is more than any one sudden experience of it.

AN: Of course. When you talk about one tree or a couple of trees or ten trees, you don't talk about the forest as a whole, because it is a big forest. Then, the parts together make the whole, in a sense, and you don't expect that it would be a minus to have a one-thousandth of the forest used for something else.

DR: You're still not answering this basic objection. Your concept of gestalt, so far as you've defined it, seems to include two things. One is that the person who is analyzing the forest, who's calculated it and determined what good the whole thing is, can come up with his own gestalt vision, and it might be one that says, "Cut the forest up into little bits." That's my gestalt vision; it's also a part of reality. The second thing your view seems to include would be anyone's negative evaluation of it, such as, "It's a swamp. Drain it. I experience it, it bothers me." You know, fix it. Turn it into something useful. That's my gestalt vision. Why is your gestalt vision that it's some sort of beautiful whole better than mine? Why should I listen to you?

AN: Well, as I say, the value of my vision is that more people have access to certain gestalt kinds, and there is more chance for wide sustainability. If they drained the swamps, there would be certain effects that are extremely dangerous ecologically, so those people who cannot get free from just one kind of negative view find it very difficult to conceive that they should save ugly places instead of beautiful ones.

DR: So you're putting forth some kind of norm that says we should be able to have as many gestalt interpretations as possible?

AN: Yes, as an instrumental norm for solving the ecological crisis.

The Lake with Motorboats

DR: So are you looking for something beautiful?

AN: Oh, not beautiful, but positive—joyful. It might not have anything to do with beauty.

DR: But you want as many joyful experiences of the place as possible.

AN: Joyful, in Spinoza's sense, yes. Where your whole personality gets engaged.

DR: OK, well, fine. I say, "We'll take this lake, down there in the distance by Ustaoset [pointing out the window, down across the *vidda*], and that half, no motorboats allowed. On this half, motorboats allowed — because we want as many possible experiences of joy." What's wrong with this argument? Would you say that would be fine?

AN: No, because there's acoustic pollution for some of those who wouldn't like motorboats. If it's a small lake, that would be very bad.

DR: But don't people have to compromise to get as many possible gestalt interpretations?

AN: Yes, but they can't inhabit the same place all the time. And you do not have the total experience when traveling at fifty, sixty, seventy miles an hour. The experience you get in a motorboat is one of velocity. One can no longer get this velocity in the street, so one turns to the pristine lakes. In ecology, we need sustainability in our search for gestalts. If we go on industrializing, we learn to look out this window and say, "Here is a part of Norway that is empty; it is nothing. I cannot see anything. It is barren. It is vacant. We must have something valuable there, like a factory." Energy abuse will still go on. In order to stabilize energy consumption in Norway, you have to have more people aware of these wonderful, essential parts of reality, which are anything but empty.

Roosevelt in Africa

DR: You have to get more people to like these places. They can't just be aware of them. They have to go out there and not say, "Nothing is here." They have to go out and exclaim, "What a beautiful place! How wonderful it is right now—leave it as it is." Not only a particular experience, but a particular way of judging that experience. Look at it this way: Teddy Roosevelt is out in Africa hunting wild game. He's shooting zebras. And he's saying, "God, I love this country. I really want to protect it!" Why does he want to protect it? Because he likes to go there and hunt zebras. If he didn't go, and couldn't go out hunting, he might not like it. For him, the experience, the gestalt, includes going out into this beautiful place and killing some animals.

AN: Sure. There are many excellent hunters who are on the deep ecology side.

DR: Right. That's how conservation began, but now these animals are considered an endangered species. You would want someone to go out there and have the experience, "These animals are so beautiful, let's not kill them." You would want them to go there and have a whole different kind of experience. And I'm not sure that the gestalt approach in itself gives you the criteria to determine this. If it does, please tell me more about it.

AN: There is a lack of high-order gestalts—landscape, for instance. I mean, wide experience, where you see a lot of features as a whole, and that demands that you are somehow more enclosed in a comprehensive gestalt. The more you connect, the more you are able to argue for not having industrial society goods everywhere. You come to see a lot of gestalts that are such that they exclude tremendous energy use, for instance.

DR: That's good. You know I like that. But what if I say that an even higher-order gestalt is all these beautiful things, and then man, here, inhabiting, killing them for sport and food.

AN: All over. All over.

DR: Not all over. Just a few hunters killing reindeer. Or what about hunting of lynx, or something that there's hardly anything of? I mean, why couldn't someone say that it's a higher-order gestalt to have . . .

AN: . . . no lynx?

DR: Well, to have, you know, a few—to hunt them. To hunt even the last one, just the experience is higher, because a human being is there. I mean, why couldn't someone argue that?

AN: Then you could have certain people who would pay a top price to be able to shoot the last tiger.

DR: Yes. You need to have some higher norms to determine which gestalts are better. You need to say something like, "If there's more biological diversity up to a certain level in this area, then that's a higher-level gestalt." Because you want to be able to say, "It's better off if we could keep these animals than to have people hunt them."

The Right and the Many

AN: But then you must already have a kind of ecological view that says diversity is a plus, like in conservation biology. Conservation biologists certainly have access to a lot of experiences of reality that are special to that group. They look for certain diversity. They look for certain organisms. They value many very ugly things, and so-called ugly landscapes. Not beautiful, but valuable; they see them and have a joyful experience of them. And the more people have a joyful experience of the ecosystem, the more chances there are to save more ecosystems than just the spectacular ones. The total view you must have is that the earth should go on. Now we have used a fantastic number of words . . .

The gestalt approach helps me and also many others. They see more. They will look out this window here and say, "Oh, here is, of course, some water, and then you have some snow, and so on."

DR: So that you would look out here and see the patches of snow and learn what that says about the previous winter. And learn how these lakes got to be where they are . . .

AN: You look with much more delight on mosses, because, in your way of conceiving, you know that the moss comes before many of these so-called beautiful flowers, and it's nice to say, "Oh, here is such-and-such flower," while others say, "No, there is just brown." Well, it is not a flower now, but just a plant. You learn to appreciate plants, rather than just flowers.

DR: You would want the kind of deepening of gestalts that comes with returning to the same place every year for thirty years . . .

AN: Again and again and again.

DR: To know the different kinds of rainbows you could have even when you just see one. That's all part of it, right?

AN: Oh, yes. And after being in a certain spot many times, you of course see very much more until it's unbelievable how much there is in any single wild place. Then, you need not go new places all the time and more and more spectacular places, enormous flowers in South America and certain celebrated places. Ecologically, spectacular nature is not important.

DR: Hmm.

AN: So speaking not about ecology, but about philosophy, the gestalt ontology hangs together with possibilities of simple means and rich ends.

DR: Mmm.

AN: I see you now have given up.

DR: (Laughs)

The young Arne stepping out into the unknown

Mina—is this who Arne still longs for?

A stoic sailing trip with Mother, 1916

*"Mother, I was playing with the ocean." On
the Riviera near the Italian border*

The family Naess. Clockwise from left: *Ragnar, Erling, Kiki, Christine, and Arne*

The young climber in Vienna, 1933

Arne climbing at Kolsås with his first wife, Else Hertzberg. "She wasn't just doing the things I liked to do. She liked them, too. At least I think she did."

Tvergastein

Door of Tvergastein

Living room, Tvergastein

"Too cold in the hut for you? Well then, let's play a little."

Camp in the Sierra Nevada, Spain

Arne climbing in the Jotunheimen

"I have learned as much from my rats as I have from Plato."

Meeting Nehru in India, with Lord and Lady Mountbatten looking on

Overlooking the fjord from the slopes of Stettind, northern Norway

At work with Spinoza high in the Hindu Kush, 1964

Below the brink of the Grand Canyon, 1988

Arne building a fire at sunset in the Arizona desert, 1988

Playing with Kit Fai Naess at the edge of deep waters, 1989

At the deep ecology center in the Tasmanian rain forest, 1989

On thin ice

IX: ON THIN ICE

N ow we are in Oslo, in the backyard of the Naess house in Skådalen. It is necessary to return to the city for Arne to remember the rest of his world, to dispel the illusion that his has been a lonely journey through books, outrageous actions, and extreme positions disliked by the authorities. Here, he thinks of the members of his family who have been important and close to him throughout his life.

The Naess family is a clan made up of extraordinary individuals. Three brothers and one sister: Ragnar, Erling, Arne, and Kiki. Each has followed a unique and somewhat surprising path, deviating from what Norwegian society would expect, but thereby unifying themselves as a true Norwegian family. Ragnar left early on for America, received a Ph.D. in chemistry from MIT, and went on to one of the first classes of the Harvard Business School. He became a successful stockbroker, married a young Communist, and later gave almost all of his money away to several educational institutions. Now over ninety, he spends most of his days playing the piano. Erling started an international shipping empire, and became famous for his role in assisting the Norwegian government in exile out of London during the war. He has funded a maritime museum in Bergen, and lives most of the time in Bermuda. Kiki married a German doctor before the war, but returned to Norway after its end to practice physical therapy for many years.

She raised her son, Arne, Jr., alone, but he looked at his uncle, our Arne Naess, as a mentor in climbing and outrageous behavior, if not the typical father figure. The nephew was inspired to imitate and then excel his uncle's wild climbing and adventuring exploits. This special relationship between the two Arnes is perhaps the closest parent-child feeling professor Arne has felt. With his own sons, Ragnar and Arild, and his daughter, Lotte, the ever-present distance has kept him somehow away. And with his first two wives, there was always the pressure of love as opposed to commitment, passion fighting friendship. Other women always tempted him away, and in both cases, he became unable to abide by society's morals in favor of his own.

Why did this pull of emotion continue to threaten the domestic life of a thinker so concerned with honesty and open, truthful communication? Perhaps because of his very need to experience emotion, if not to express it in words to others. He was startled that he was not sad enough when his younger son Arild died in an accident while only in his twenties. This did not faze Arne as much as it might have, and he continued to crave extremes of emotion, even though this went against his intellectual predilections and theories. His love affairs made him suffer immensely, for reasons that come out here, yet one feels that he enjoyed the ability to feel obsessed or intoxicated, full of beauty, not responsibility. He was not interested in judgment, or evaluation of the situation—just the continued realization of the largest sense of Self.

Arne's wealthy and successful brothers have always offered him assistance, particularly when he does not ask for it. Extolling the virtues of the simple life, he gets to fly to exotic and wild places whenever these two, and more recently his nephew, Arne, Jr.—now fabulously successful in business in his own right—choose to invite him. It is, of course, difficult to refuse such generosity. But how does it affect a man whose maxim is said to be "Simple in means, rich in ends"? Once again, there is an allusion to Gandhi, who is reputed to have said, "It costs many people a lot of money to keep me living in poverty." The Naess family has respected Arne's need to be different. And they have helped make this desire a reality.

We move on to consider the continued pain of thought, and the difficulty of coming to conclusions in life. But speculation must, for each of us, come to an end at last. And, yet, how can we be sure? "Life," wrote Arne's friend, the novelist, Jens Bjørneboe, "is like running on thin ice." The same slippery questions remain, even as they cut sharp swaths in the surface. Does the vague communicate more than the precise? Does the sobriety of detachment get closer to the truth than emotional contact? Here we are, sitting in the garden, in the warm summer sun, butterflies in the air, each of them competing for Arne's attention as something to identify with in nature. How is it all changing, now that he is eighty years old?

The Net of Security

AN: We have not enough about my family . . .

DR: Well, let's go back. Your brothers?

AN: In the thirties, my brother Erling made it big in the tanker business, and in shipping, whaling, and other things. He was interested in me as a younger brother in a very nice way, completely respecting my decision to go into philosophy, but at the same time, highly skeptical about how I could support myself being a philosopher. I was skeptical as well. Erling was completely willing and able to get me into business. He would say, "You could even climb more than you do, because we can see to it that you get as many vacations as you wish." He himself was not a climber, but a wanderer.

He was always an influence in telling me that life should be planned; life should be rational, you should have reasons for things you do, and you should arrange your life in such a way that you can follow your interests. It was very much a self-realization ideal, but rather egocentric and family centered, not the great Self I came to speak of later. The generosity was, first of all, within the family, not in any other sense. Politics and all these social questions were considered silly and not worthy of attention. He would often invite me fantastic places with him. He was more than a close friend, but something like the father I never had, in the sense of being older and saying, "I have much more experience than you have." So he certainly helped me in life, especially before the war, and my other brother, Ragnar, did also, though he had already gone to the United States in the twenties, never to return. When I started going to America in '38, I often visited him, and he also showed me how you could live a life with a lot of possibilities I didn't have, because, with his money, he could buy wonderful sailing boats, he could go to concerts as much as he wished, he could have tremendously good teachers give him piano lessons—and he showed this warmth toward me, lending me money occasionally, and otherwise acting as a great positive force.

DR: So your brothers certainly made life easier for you?

AN: Yes, they gave me a feeling of security. In welfare countries, we speak about the "security net"—if something bad happens to you, if you really need and cannot afford help, the state exists to protect you—and those two brothers were a kind of security net for me. They would ask me what I needed, and I always answered, "Everything is OK." To my richest brother, Erling, I started saying very early on, "I am rich. My finances are like a granite cliff of security." And he would laugh. But I would insist that if he was going to support me, I never pressed him to do it, even if I said, "All is in order."

DR: They continue to help you now.

AN: Yes. And they, of course, had a much better relationship with my mother in the thirties, but what had happened in infancy still had major influence—this distance, this *Panzercharakter*, all this we have spoken about. I never had the usual, Norwegian kind of family feeling. Only the nearness of these brothers meant the most to me.

But already in the thirties, I think I saw my sister, Kiki, as a successful kind of human being, in the sense that she showed great joy in making others joyful. She had very early on a joy from doing good to others. So I have called her, very often, the most successful human being in the Naess family. In her work as a physical therapist, she encouraged her patients, saying, "Good, good." And she would laugh afterward, saying, "This was the most preposterous movement he made, but it was just a little better than before. And I said, 'Marvelous, marvelous!' " And they did things they never before were able to do. This convinced me that on the whole, people need encouragement, though sometimes, absolutely, they should be put down. But mostly, they need encouragement.

DR: So you, too, tended to encourage your students and other people?

AN: I tried, yes, absolutely. Yes. But I cannot be compared to my sister, no. Not at all. I was, after all, called the *lyslukker*, the candle snuffer. I admired my sister very much in her ability to spur people on.

Her son, Arne, Jr., was very much like a son to me, and in the forties I had a lot more fun with him, because I could be myself, doing things that my younger children couldn't easily participate in. As Arne, Jr., has grown up and become successful in business and in climbing and in all else, he has shown a kind of gratefulness for the time we spent together when he was young. I was always with him joyfully, trying to be a proper friend, but never motivated by any moralistic concern or feeling of duty. We have never been at all sentimental toward each other, despite all the wild and crazy adventures we have enjoyed together. Both he and my brother Erling have respected my academic life, though it is far away from their worlds of business.

DR: Just the other day, you said how interested Erling was in hearing you talk about the wonders of nature.

AN: Yes, he was quite interested in a very touching way. Again and again, he would ask for more, especially when I said we need to save the earth from what humankind is doing. He couldn't really understand quite what I was after. But he understood the notion of distances in the universe and that it's bad that Einstein has made us more or less sure that we can't have any communication with all those galaxies that are getting farther and farther away from us, and so on. He wished to have more talk, much more talk.

DR: But, at the same time, it isn't really information you're giving them, as much as an attitude, a kind of questioning?

AN: Well, he hasn't used his imagination in this way as a businessman, and he has an imagination as I have an imagination. It's a good deep feeling when he uses his imagination in these new areas. I say things that appeal to his sense of strangeness, his lust for faraway things, and he likes it. So I never felt that I don't give back some of what they give to me. But I am touched when they are so eager and willing to do good things for me, as now Arne has done these last years. The Naess family somehow has good internal relations, which not every successful family has. We are very close friends. The friendships are the longest we have, so there is a difference. But the difference is that these friendships are as old as we are, and can hardly be distinguished from the extent of our own lives and selves.

The Pain of Thought

DR: You have reached your eightieth birthday, and are still as restless as ever, running up mountains, bicycling into the hills, and camping out in the desert for weeks on end. The rest of us think you haven't aged at all, but is there anything important that seems to have changed for you?

AN: Yes. So many people say that they feel as young as ever and they're as active as ever and that they don't at all feel that they are old. I think I have had, since I was sixty, at least ten or fifteen things to say about how I experience the process of aging. Physically, it's completely clear, especially if I go climbing a little where I've not climbed before. I am a fraction of my former self, especially the strength, but also the balance, when you don't have anything to hold on to with your hands but only small holds for your feet—then, of course, with balance getting weak, you fall backward. Physical, but also mental, difference. The time it takes to change an opinion, to change an attitude in research, takes longer and longer. Names disappear to some extent, and the memories of what you have just done the same day are harder to hold on to than the distant past.

When I lecture, I start a sentence where I know that in the middle of the sentence, there will be a name or an important word that I will not get hold of in time before I reach the end of the sentence. So I then have to change the sentence! This I can do and not feel bad about it. I might, for instance, stop before the name and say, "According to . . ." and then I make a gesture to indicate that the audience should tell the name. And if I do it two or three times, I can have the joke that the audience understands I have forgotten the name. So all these things together should make me feel bad, but I don't get upset at all. I think it helped me to reinforce a certain attitude through reading about Churchill's last ten years—the thick book by his favorite doctor—when once, rather far into his illness, he not only stepped out of his bed by himself but also got his slippers on by himself. And then he made a victory sign. As far as I can see, that might have been just as well done as some of his diplomatic feats during the Second World War.

In short, I think we have, at different stages of life, certain cards. It's like in bridge, where you have to play your cards well. Old age means that you get worse and worse cards, in many ways. Then you must take the victories in relation to what cards you have. When I had arteriosclerosis in my joints and couldn't even get into a car or easily get up from the bathtub, it was interesting to explore what I could still do. And I found out that climbing, where there are no holds at all and you must step with tiny steps, was possible, so my nephew, Arne, Jr., with his exceptional consideration of my situation, found a very good climb nearby, with certain points six and other points five, all of it on a slight slope. That worked very well, but I couldn't move between boulders; it was very difficult.

So it is extremely interesting to see how certain things that are considered very elementary are absolutely impossible, and other things that are considered highly difficult are still possible. You can never know what you are able to do. You never know when you get some new bad cards how you can manipulate your play such that you can get very good things out of the deficiencies. What is important is how you can transform weaknesses into strengths. For instance, if you have as a boy or girl a tendency to gather stones, that could lead into, say, a talent for gathering money. And if you are able to do that, then you can give away a lot of money.

DR: Do you feel that lifelong problems are being resolved, lifelong directions are being realized, culminated? Is it a continuous Self-realization?

AN: It is continuous, yes. I never have the impression that something is resolved, especially in research, and therefore I never throw away all the drafts where I stopped in some kind of problem, because I feel so sure I'll come back. When a book is published, I immediately make a lot of corrections in it. In the case of my textbooks of logic and methodology and philosophy, there were always new editions where I had made changes, and then certain people said, "Well, this eleventh edition of your logic is worse than all the ten before."

DR: I'm sure you will refuse to stop trying to revise this text as well! It is as if the books you write are not finished works, but rather steps on the way.

AN: I have never had the impression that they are anything more than that. Life is a process. Going strong is joyful all the way. You just do things until you have practically no power. Death is not experienced—you are only aware of the moments before death where you, let's say, have the knowledge that you are going to die the same day, but you don't experience the end at all.

DR: You're sure of this?

AN: Yes, I feel certain about that, and I would be very astonished if I changed my opinion, but I have changed many opinions, so I cannot be entirely sure about anything. Death is not a problem in the sense that I am not going to experience it. What's terrible is that others die, not that I die. I have experience of the death of others, but not of my own.

DR: And why is that terrible?

AN: I find it terrible to have this certainty that my best friends and my young son Arild are just something in the memory of certain people, and those people are fewer and fewer, and after a while there is absolutely nothing left—they are gone completely. That, I think, is a terrible thought, a really serious minus in life.

DR: Have any of the various philosophies and cultures that you've studied, with their ideas about things that happen after death, been appealing to you, or is this something just not to think about?

AN: Yes, I had great interest, but looking at the arguments for and the arguments against, the arguments against are, for me, very much stronger. If I had an experience of the same kind, I'm sure I would believe, but I haven't had an experience of that kind.

I've had acquaintances, especially a professor of moral theology, Johan Hygens, who is also an artist, and I said to him, "How can you, for instance, preach in a church about original sin? How is it possible for you? Sin?" So he said, "This is not much of a problem. Humans are such that they never reach their ideal and they feel badly, they feel guilty, about not reaching their ideals. That is an inherent property of humankind. And that's the essence of the dogma of original sin." And I said, "What? But in church you don't say it in exactly the same way as you told me." And he said, "No, of course not. I have to express this through the traditional way to an audience that has certain capacities of thinking and who are not professors of philosophy." And then I gaped and said, "Aha!"

DR: Now, would you suggest to him that he tell it to the people like it is?

AN: No, because this term "like it is" I do not recognize at all. I see the indefinite plurality of interpretation of a deep kind of experience that cannot be codified. If you have a sufficiently wide and deep perspective, then there is this indefinite and unlimited plurality . . .

DR: But at the same time, you believe in precision in language, correct? And you think that this accuracy is important to explain to all kinds of people?

AN: You cannot have a high level of preciseness all the time, because then you never get to say anything very important, which must start with something very imprecise.

DR: Why do you think that is?

AN: I think that thinking is painful, as I said before, and on the whole we talk with very little thought. When there's talk going on in one's brain, one may be led to some intuitions that are spontaneously expressed by some kind of sentence. That would be a very primitive or crude kind of sentence from the theory of preciseness and thinking, but it may be crucially important to keep it, because it was so near the intuition that it may be very deep and important for you. So when Pascal had his great illumination, he said "Feu!" and then he jumped rather fast to the expression "Dieu," and then at last "Dieu d'Abraham et Isaac!" It would be very interesting if he had had five stages before he expressed his sentence, because "Feu!" is a kind of one-word sentence with an exclamation mark. It was a little too fast that he got into a very definite, ideological, traditional interpretation of an initially inspired and intuitive sentence.

DR: Because he would have communicated more if he had been slower?

AN: Oh, yes. And it would have been more interesting for us today.

DR: We would have to figure out what he meant.

AN: Yes. Pascal limited the significance of his experience by saying too much about it. You have an intuition, something that you know is extremely important for you, for the rest of your life, even, and what exactly did you experience? If you then can hold it open, very far open, and try to relive the experience as authentically as possible, then make as much as possible out of it, you would not fall into a kind of sack where you are caught.

DR: So this means that the more words you put on an experience, the more the experience is constrained?

AN: Of course. I think so. My term "identification" comes, I think, from a particular experience, when I was looking through a microscope down on a little chemical transformation in a drop of acid, probably; then, a flea from a lemon that was also on my table but was not joining in my experiments jumped from the lemon onto the microscope and got too near to the drop and was caught. As you know, the force on the surface of the drop is too strong, and I had this terrible experience: It was like being trapped in an enormous chewing gum or something. And I knew it was impossible to save him, but instead of giving up the experiment and killing the flea fast, I was absorbed in looking at it, the movement of the legs, and its fight was so like a human being hit by something, fighting for life. I saw it completely as a human death-fight; there was no difference. I know that their nervous system is irrelevant in this case, but the identification was very strong, and it made me not want to give up a formulation like, "All life is one."

DR: Once again, I wonder if it's not somehow easier for you to identify with life forms that are very distant from your own.

AN: Yes. There is a certain distance that makes it easier to understand nonviolence, so that I can be a very good interpreter of Gandhi, in spite of lacking his nearness to conflicts. I have, in a shameful way, no strong urge to get into the center of them . . .

DR: "Seek the center of the conflicts!" is one of your norms, no?

AN: Seek the center of the conflicts! If there is something awkward happening, or something socially risky, I keep away from it, but will then talk about it, read about it, write about it. One has to have a tremendous social capacity for joining other people and struggling. But facing opponents is getting easier for me because of the distance I have from humanity. This also means I am rarely among those who are fighting deliberately.

DR: It's also the same kind of distance that's part of the objectivity of science: Don't get too involved in what you study. Yet, at the same time, you want to identify with creatures like the flea that are very distant from human experience and scale. It's kind of curious.

AN: Well, in research I think, I have had great joy from experiments. For instance, when I was testing the use of the term "certain" among people, it was a great joy to be with them and see how they used the term. I gave them glasses of water and said, "This is a very weak solution," and they would ask, "Which solution of water is it?" I am a participant in research, and I love the relation to what I am investigating if it has to do with nature. With the flowers at Tvergastein, I note down all the changes in their morphology, doing plant ecology in an entirely amateurish way. I've never felt that I have a cold relation to the themes of my research. I am near when I am doing research.

DR: But at the same time, the things you identify with are those that you investigate, rather than some kind of immediate empathy with life around you. It's things far away that you choose to concentrate on.

AN: Yes, far away, in the sense that tiny things going on near my cottage are extremely far away from what most human beings would consider important. I am involved especially, with greatest pleasure, trying to find the smallest specimen of a certain plant that grows near my hut. The distance comes in a rather complicated way. Sometimes it's near, if far from the maddening crowds.

DR: It's the tiny life forms that are close to you and your life, rather than the sufferings of people in other parts of the world or in your own country. It's not human struggle that you choose to identify with.

AN: When I have had to do with human suffering, I cannot stand it many weeks. In 1945, at this office for people who disappeared during the war, I had to deal with torturers and fathers and mothers who were completely distraught. I have not the nerves even to be in grave social work, where you are up to your knees in tragedy.

I ask myself, "How can you use so much of your time and energy on these things when your own species has such terrible problems?" I was for many years in the peace movement. There is something there, something strange. It is so much more difficult for me to deal with the confusions of humanity.

DR: But it's as if it also spreads over into your philosophy of semantics and language. You don't think the most communicative kind of language is where people are talking a lot or saying very specific things, but when generalizations are put out, vague utterances that sort of suggest the direction of the message. You believe that's somehow deeper because it's more general.

AN: Certainly I have a tendency toward generalizations. I'm not a storyteller, and like so many other philosophers especially of the European kind, broad statements are very important for me. You are right there.

DR: In your whole theory of preciseness, you're saying a somewhat controversial thing, that somehow vague statements say more than more specific ones. They allow more possible interpretations in different directions and, therefore, they have this profound place in communication, whereas others would just say, "This is vague, it's a slogan, it's not enough."

AN: Well, I was very influenced in my semantics through reading the history of physics and mathematics, and there, for instance, they could use the term "proof" for seven thousand years and there's an idea there that is extremely ambiguous and vague. So that through the centuries, it has been interpreted differently, all the time. The so-called Law of the Conservation of Energy was formulated 150 years ago—there's an idea that is extremely important, but it's very vague and ambiguous and nobody has really found a good formulation of it. What they do is that when it's disproved, they transform the disconfirmation into a confirmation with the Law of the Constancy of Energy—just adding one new energy, they get constancy again. This is, of course, cheating, semantically. But it's very good science.

DR: So science has something against semantics?

AN: There is a lot of important use of ambiguous and vague formulations in the history of science, but it's not often acknowledged. In the popular view, it seems that we get to know more and more about temperature, for instance, or energy, or a term like "time." These are continually being redefined. One feels the pain, and there are certainly no easy solutions anywhere.

DR: Why is thinking painful?

AN: It is a strain on having a good time. You don't have a good time while thinking.

DR: So it's not automatic.

AN: No, far from it. I can experience when we are talking in these sessions that, from time to time, you open some questions for me which I feel absolutely should be thought about a little deeper before I talk. But I still just go on talking . . .

DR: Speech doesn't always demand thought.

AN: Some people, I am glad to say, stop talking, and you see them really wrestle with their thoughts. That's very nice. With the brain humans have, it is easy for us to get away from any kind of so-called life importance and get lost in ideas.

DR: It's easier? I thought it was painful.

AN: It's painful if you try to press them to think more difficult thoughts.

DR: But you think the movement toward the abstract and unsolvable is very basic to the human being.

AN: Yes, I think it is to some extent common to all the more successful mammals. My rats in California also enjoyed problems. But in humans, this has developed enormously, leading us quickly to the unsolvable and marginal problems, far away and intangible. Our brain is most unique, compared to any other organ or beings on this planet . . .

DR: More unique than the brain of rats?

AN: Yes. But we shouldn't be at all condescending toward rats. One should admit that mammals like rats have a deep sense of inquiry. They will sniff around rather than eat, even if they are very hungry. Even a person dying of starvation may do the same.

Difference

DR: How have you helped others in teaching them to think? How does the vagueness help?

AN: Think of what we are doing now in these sessions. If something of this is written down, could it help anybody to read what I have been saying? I think it could, but probably just a small minority of humanity who feel outside, who feel they are different. There are many who say, "I've always felt different. It was difficult for me to adapt because I felt different." I certainly felt very different, but I was happy to get some self-confidence very early, so I never felt there was something deeply wrong with the differences I felt from others. One of the messages is, of course, that you don't at all feel that being different is any kind of minus in general. Difference can be positive. According to Spinoza, you can make this difference tolerable for others and, therefore, tolerable for yourself.

DR: Is it something to be made tolerable or is it something to exploit, to assert to the world?

AN: Well, I was talking about being different not as a negative thing, even if others find it a negative thing. When it really comes to a question of this, I try to say, "By God, you are on a par with anybody else and you are different, but this is within the human range of differences, and you will find others who are different in approximately the same way, and you will have a good feeling for what you are." On the radio, I have said this: "Everybody should feel equal to Einstein and Leonardo da Vinci *as human beings,* unique and infinitely rich."

I don't know how I got that feeling, but when I am together with one human being in the mountains or in other situations where we get close, I never have any feeling that certain people are boring or that certain people don't have an inner life. If they were able to articulate exactly what they were experiencing, then, of course, it would be a book of great importance.

DR: But if the other person up there in the mountains talks too much, you have been known to get upset.

AN: I have a technique to go into deep quarters very fast, to the limits; I go to the limits practically immediately.

DR: In a conversation?

AN: Yes. I won't put up with small talk at all.

DR: Right. But if the person wants to talk too much and does not leave any space, then you might not have such a good time . . .

AN: Well, it's very easy to stop them, I find. It's very easy to stop them with certain questions: "How do you conceive the present situation between us? If someone has a need to speak to somebody, how do you explain this need to speak?" It can be said in a nice way, smiling and so on. If we're going to go all the way to the summit together . . .

I once met a man in the Austrian Alps, far away, and we were walking along the same mountain path. He was for Hitler and for annexation of Austria—it was back in the thirties. I did not, of course, agree. And then it was, of course, very easy to get to deep things, because I made my point clear, but without any kind of aggression.

DR: And how did he react?

AN: Very well. He said, "All right, you are a Social Democrat from Scandinavia. Your problems are so different from our problems."

DR: So he didn't give anything in his position?

AN: Not much, I think, but he did give a little, because he'd not met anyone who had this kind of serious approach in talking.

DR: He, too, was interested in the difference.

AN: Yes. I think it made an impression on him. Of course, I couldn't convince him of something opposite from what he'd believed for years. I never expect to convince, only to make people less certain about things that I dislike—that, I think, is very important. Therefore, I asked in the United States when they once arranged lectures for me—"I would like to speak to the Daughters of the American Revolution"—to have some audience that would really take issue with what I had to say.

DR: And did you do it?

AN: They couldn't arrange that, but they said, "There are certain lawyers who are just as reactionary and impossible." And that was arranged. I talked against this very famous so-called father of the hydrogen bomb, Edward Teller, who was also a fabulous teacher and a very great influence at that time. I made a straightforward Gandhian analysis of the hydrogen bomb. They were so conservative that, because I was a foreign scholar, they didn't attack me really badly at all. They had a polite discussion. Instead, they attacked the man who had arranged my lecture, and that was not polite. Even that attempt was completely unsuccessful in finding an audience that would really throw tomatoes at me.

DR: Well, people don't really get angry with you. Have you noticed that?

AN: Yes.

DR: I think it has to do with the manner in which you present ideas so that they appear so amusing. Even if people disagree, they won't want to get upset with this playful fellow with this gentle way. On the other hand, you do have a tendency to walk away when you're done and not actually listen to your adversaries. And that might not be such a positive trait in the end.

AN: Yes, they disliked that in 1968. In the student social revolution, I was slippery in a way that I didn't seem to take it all very seriously. That was bad, of course. But I'm glad they told me that. And I said, "Of course, but I'm here now to have a real talk with you, a real debate." "OK, we shall have a real conflict." But I didn't succeed in getting into a really uncomfortable, ugly kind of fight with them.

DR: Have you ever gotten into such debates?

AN: Yes, I think so. But then I tend to stop them very early.

DR: Not wanting to press forward for the truth or just not liking the method?

AN: I don't know. I try to terminate it somehow by a conclusion that we are completely at odds at this point.

DR: But usually, you try to get people to admit that they actually agree with you. At least, these days.

AN: Yes. They believe they disagree, but that is an illusion.

DR: You want them to admit that they are, in fact, on your side.

Cautionary Tales

DR: Is there anything that you would caution about yourself? I mean, is there anything that you would wish to be different?

AN: Oh, yes. Many things, certainly. I would gladly—yes, sure. First of all, this distance, this *Panzercharakter*, is still there. I still live too much in my own world. This is worst when it compromises the norms of friendship. A couple of people have complained, saying that when they were in real trouble, I was not very helpful. Even if I might worry a lot about their situation, I was not very helpful, whereas others, like my sister, Kiki, would be far more considerate. There are many things I could find, which are deplorable, I would say. Yes. That's a tremendous lot you've got there.

DR: (Laughs)

AN: But as a motto for most of my life, I would say that the search for a recognition of wonder has been most rewarding.

DR: So you were not most engaged in solving philosophical problems as much as enjoying the questions?

AN: That is also weakness. That is a real weakness. But seeing this is—ha ha—what I am doing is not at all solving the problem. It is just a skirmish, like I am just walking around on the shore, and you have this ocean, and the same holds in philosophy. It is fine to walk along the shore, but some people, like Spinoza, really go into the ocean. Yet, there is nothing in Spinoza I would say is definitive, nothing. People imagine I find solutions in Spinoza. I don't feel any solution in Spinoza.

DR: Right. But you would not like to find solutions. Or would you?

AN: I don't know what it would mean to find one. I can't see the difference between being completely convinced on a Saturday and finding a solution. Here I am, completely convinced on Saturday after working on this thing all week, or all year. By Monday, I will start finding some flaws. So much for solution.

I haven't had this marvellous experience of being both completely convinced and convinced that it is the truth. How can truth be reached? How can knowledge be attained? That was my one and only lecture at Cambridge. I said we cannot see finding truth as getting nearer and nearer. But if you like to hear a kind of definition that would be useful for certain purposes, I would say that it is so. And that I have from maybe a housewife or a couple of schoolchildren or someone from my early questionnaire research in *"Truth" as Conceived by Those Who Are Not Professional Philosophers*. That it is so. And that, what does that solve? Nothing.

DR: But you don't get Self-realization. You separated that from truth.

AN: Oh, yes. I don't use the term "truth" there. Self-realization is also a process. People ask me, "What's the maximum of Self-realization?" and I then offer them some kind of mystical sentence, a mystic's unity with the whole, but it doesn't appeal to me to try to find out what I mean by that. Or, I say that ultimately or fundamentally, all living beings are one, but what could the full consequences of this really be? But I stick to such a formulation. There's something there that disappears if you try to be more precise. Something elusive . . .

DR: Is that so with any sentence? Do you lose something when you try and make it more precise?

AN: Very many sentences are said with a feeling of being intuitively true and important, with a certain spontaneity. Then, it is difficult to improve upon them by trying to be more precise. And this is enough.

DR: Well, we already have thirty hours on tape!

AN: Well, then . . .

DR: Enough!

AN: Let's eat. Yes.

EPILOGUE:
A WALK IN THE WORLD OF JOY

When Arne Naess got hold of these manuscript pages, he took out his red pen and set to work. Hardly any paragraph escaped unscathed. "That's not what I meant!" he cried. "This you must qualify—it will be misunderstood." No one should be offended by the text. No blatant or crass statement should remain. Arne proceeded to try to turn the conversations into fodder for philosophical articles, each point introduced with utmost care, every assertion qualified and refined until it would make sense only to those well versed in the terminology, deep inside the structures of the thinker's mind.

Well, I told him, this will never wash. What I have tried to present here is the unwritten Arne Naess—not the meticulous, point-by-point analyst whose byzantine paths of thought remain incomprehensible to the uninitiated. I was after the reluctant raconteur, the man whose childhood resistance to his mother's love of language sent him reeling into logic, only to bounce back with flowing tales of wanderings across a wide world of mountains, climbed or inaccessible, inside and outside the limits of the Self.

Here is the Arne Naess whom readers of his work may not have known: someone who weaves from topic to event, principle to memory, so in love with precision yet refusing to give any concept a fast definition. Why not? Its ability to inspire should never be reduced. Besides, it is painful to think.

In mixing and matching, assembling and paring down our discussions, I've been led to consider deeper questions about Arne's life, further footholds on the routes of his philosophy, those untold rope lengths now discarded far below the summit of a secure Self. I came to the conclusion that, for a man trained in the exactness of the analytical trend of twentieth-century philosophy, the jump to a deep ecological consciousness is a long one indeed. Those philosophers schooled in the analysis of sentences upon logical grounds look for the truth content of a proposition in the precise connection of the words used. They are descended from that group of thinkers Arne fraternized with in the cafés and classrooms of Vienna. But as we have seen, this was a movement that Arne could only stomach for the first thirty years of his life. Afterward, he spent his time trying to distance himself from the belief that language really could be the ultimate arbiter of precision.

Here is a philosopher with a love-hate relationship with precision, a suspicion of rhetoric, and a deep respect for poetry — maybe not poetic language, but poetic action. Beautiful actions, not moral ones. The poetry of life, proven in these pages to be so much more than the refinement of articulation.

Arne may have much more in common with Ludwig Wittgenstein than he would like to admit. Wittgenstein was hero to the logical empiricists, yet his life and work really celebrate the ambiguities they dreamed of overcoming. His earliest ruminations, enumerated point by point in the *Tractatus,* end with the following suggestion: These propositions are like a ladder used to reach a higher plane. Once you get there, you throw away the ladder, and you no longer need the words. You have moved beyond the discourse.

The dream of a world of facts ends up being much more than its measured image. At its summit is a kind of crystalline joy. By dividing the world up, one reaches a place where language cannot help you anymore, where nothing more can be said, and all must be lived.

The analytic philosophers tried to shirk Wittgenstein's mysticism, but to all astute readers it remains. So, too, with Arne Naess, who retains anecdote and art even as he tries to spurn them — especially in these roving ascents of thought he has tried to cross out with his red pen. The tension comes, I believe, not from any uncertainty in how to act and think, but in the unshakable richness of experience that so eludes description, even for the most learned of philosophers.

These are, as you have read, experiences motivated by a felt distance from the rest of humanity. But they are friendly expansions of the self, brought forth through identification with the farthest reaches of the living worlds. The suffering of paramecia. The extinction of the dinosaurs. The big bang. Humanity, according to Naess, was there. Yet, these are connections that words do not know. No matter how beautiful, no matter how clear. We are of the same kind. Do not speak. Listen, and pay no attention to the words.

This is why he is so silent as we descend the mountain ridges from Tvergastein, why he does not speak as our car speeds down the highway back to Oslo or through the Arizona high desert, in search of a perfect place so ordinary that none of us will be able to remember it. Live there. Dwell in the land—do not even imagine you will be able to explain what it was like.

Unless. Unless the way we talk about ourselves and nature is reformed from the outset. Here, Arne's message leads closer to the second major stream of twentieth-century philosophy, something called phenomenology, associated with Husserl and Heidegger, whose slogan is "Back to the things themselves!" Learn to describe the world as it directly appears, before science, before logic, before subjects and objects, parts, and wholes. A nature of appearances, shadows, tendencies, and movements, and a humanity that is also these same things. Arne claims no special kinship with this sect, as they too, in their attempt to articulate the aforementioned vision fall sway to a baroque terminology as arbitrary as any other game played with language. But he likes the slogan: Let the world come to you and discover you cannot leave it. You are wedded to it forever, before and beyond the partings of birth and death.

No wonder Naess refuses to define his concepts. No surprise this precision is all part of the play. In the beginning is the step in the sand. And the footprint that never blows away. The forest is human even as we first see it, even before we call it a forest, long before we dream of cutting down even one tree to use in any way. The seeds of the human world are already there in our first glance. Neither earth nor humanity comes first, if we are unable to imagine one without the other.

One night in Santa Cruz, I take Arne down to see the breeding ground of the California elephant seals. The sun poised on the horizon, we dash down the sandy path of human footprints to be sure to reach the site before nightfall. Crossing rangers' barricades, ignoring large signs that cautioned "Warning: Wild elephant seals!" we run on, against the law, as the sun disappears. The trail is much longer than either of us had imagined. It becomes difficult to see beyond our feet and the wall of the sand dunes that seem to envelop us more completely the closer we come to the sea. The path begins to dissipate into the surrounding sand, and bellows of joy are heard more and more frequently from beyond the hills topped with darkening grasses, swishing in the wind. Finally, we round a bend to emerge on a landscape of only white sand, and see to the left a tiny ephemeral pool, full of huge, frolicking animals, smiling in the night. They rise and plummet, submerging themselves, only to surge up again into the air, murmuring happy sounds. It is almost dark now—the rich, deep blue of the Pacific dusk. Arne leaves the trail, heads west over the crest toward the ocean. He saunters with the firm but ragged gait of a man in the prime of his life, almost eighty years old, veteran of mountain paths far and near. He walks with conviction, appearing at once tough and fragile beneath the night sky. As he moves into his beloved distance, pausing to stand in the sand, it is harder to make out the division between the man and the world. He remains motionless, like some lone, sturdy tree with its white hair crazy with wind. Beside him lie two sleeping giant seals. They do not notice the intruder, his identity so fused with theirs in the darkness that there is no line. The world emerges and looks at the world, only to return to it once and for all in the end. Night falls on the beach of Año Nuevo, and the philosopher and nature are one.

SELECTED WORKS BY ARNE NAESS

The printed output of Arne Naess is extraordinarily prolific in Norwegian and English, with a few entries in French and German. I have limited the following chronological list to works that seem most representative of the man's thought through the various periods of his life depicted in this book. For an exhaustive list until 1982, see Arne Naess, "How My Philosophy Seemed to Develop," in *Philosophers on Their Own Work* (1983). After that, particularly on deep ecology, see Warwick Fox, *Toward a Transpersonal Ecology* (1990).

Erkenntnis und wissenschaftliches Verhalten. Oslo: Norwegian Academy of Sciences, Inaugural Dissertation no. 1, 1936.

"Common Sense and Truth." *Theoria* 4 (1938), pp. 39-58.

"Truth" as Conceived by Those Who Are Not Professional Philosophers. Oslo: Jacob Dybwad, 1939.

Interpretation and Preciseness: A Contribution to the Theory of Communicative Action. Oslo: Norwegian Academy of Sciences, 1953.

With Jens Christophersen and Kjell Kvalø. *Democracy, Ideology, and Objectivity*. Oslo: Universitetsforlaget, 1956.

"La validité de normes fundamentales." *Logic et Analyse* 1, no. 1 (1958), pp. 4-13.

"The Inquiring Mind. Notes on the Relation between Philosophy and Science." *Inquiry* 4 (1961), pp. 162-89.

"Reflections about Total Views." *Philosophy and Phenomenological Research* 25 (1964), pp. 16-29.

Gandhi and the Nuclear Age. Totowa, N.J.: Rowman, 1965.

"Science as Behavior: Prospects and Limitations of a Behavioural Metascience." In *Scientific Psychology*, ed. B. Wolman and E. Nagel. New York: Basic Books, 1965.

Communication and Argument. Oslo: Universitetsforlaget, 1966.

"Sanskrit for Generalister" (Sanskrit for generalists). Mimeograph. Oslo: Institute for Philosophy, 1967.

Scepticism. London: Humanities Press, 1968.

Four Modern Philosophers: Carnap, Wittgenstein, Heidegger, Sartre. Chicago: University of Chicago Press, 1968.

"Kierkegaard and the Values of Education." *Journal of Value Inquiry* 2 (1969), pp. 196-200.

The Pluralist and Possibilist Aspect of the Scientific Enterprise. Oslo: Universitetsforlaget, 1972.

"The Shallow and the Deep, Long-Range Ecology Movements: A Summary." *Inquiry* 16 (1973), pp. 95-100.

"The Place of Joy . . . in a World of Fact." *North American Review* 258, no. 2 (1973), pp. 53-57.

Gandhi and Group Conflict: An Exploration of Satyagraha—Theoretical Background. Oslo: Universitetsforlaget, 1974.

Dialog with A. J. Ayer. "Is the Glass on the Table?" In *Reflexive Water: The Basic Concerns of Mankind*, ed. Fons Elders. London: Souvenir Press, 1974.

"The Case against Science." In *Science between Culture and Counter-Culture*, ed. C. J. Dessauer. Nijmegen: Dekker & Van de Vegt, 1975, pp. 25-48.

Freedom, Emotion, and Self-Subsistence: A Systematization of a Part of Spinoza's Ethics. Oslo: Universitetsforlaget, 1975.

"Spinoza and Ecology." *Philosophia* 7, no. 1 (1977), pp. 45-54.

"Notes on the Methodology of Normative Systems." *Methodology and Science* 10 (1977), pp. 64-79.

"Self-Realization in Mixed Communities of Humans, Bears, Sheep, and Wolves." *Inquiry* 22 (1979), pp. 231-41.

"Modesty and the Conquest of Mountains." In *The Mountain Spirit*, ed. Michael Tobias and Harold Drasdo. New York: Overlook Press, 1979, pp. 13-16.

With Jon Hellesnes. "Norway." In *Handbook of World Philosophy since 1945*, ed. John Burr. Westport, Conn.: Greenwood Press, 1980.

"Simple in Means, Rich in Ends: A Conversation with Arne Naess." *Ten Directions*, Summer/Fall 1982, pp. 7-12.

"How My Philosophy Seemed to Develop." In *Philosophers on Their Own Work*, vol. 10, ed. André Mercier and Maja Svilar. New York: Peter Lang, 1983.

"A Defense of the Deep Ecology Movement." *Environmental Ethics* 6, no. 3 (1984), pp. 265-70.

"Intuition, Intrinsic Value, and Deep Ecology: Comments on an Article by Warwick Fox." *Ecologist* 14, no. 5/6 (1984), pp. 201-3.

"Identification as a Source for Deep Ecological Attitudes." In *Deep Ecology*, ed. Michael Tobias. San Diego: Avant Books, 1985.

"The World of Concrete Contents." *Inquiry* 28 (1985), pp. 417-28.

"Intrinsic Value: Will the Defenders of Nature Please Rise?" *Conservation Biology*, ed. Michael Soulé. Sunderland, Mass.: Sinauer Associates, 1985.

"Consequences of an Absolute *No* to Nuclear War." In *Nuclear Weapons and the Future of Humanity*, ed. Avner Cohen and Steven Lee. Totowa, N.J.: Rowman and Allanheld, 1986.

"Philosophy of Wolf Policies (Part I)." *Conservation Biology* 1, no. 1 (1987), pp. 396-409.

"The Basics of Deep Ecology." *Resurgence*, no. 126 (January 1988), pp. 4-7.

"Self-Realization: An Ecological Approach to Being in the World." *Thinking Like a Mountain*, ed. Joanna Macy and John Seed. Santa Cruz: New Society Publishers, 1988.

"Deep Ecology and Ultimate Premises." *Ecologist* 18 (1988), pp. 128-31.

"Sustainable Development and the Deep Long-Range Ecology Movement." *Trumpeter* 5 (1988), pp. 138-42.

"Metaphysics of the Treeline." *Appalachia*, June 1989, pp. 56-59.

"The Deepness of Deep Ecology." *Earth First!* December 1989, p. 32.

With David Rothenberg. *Ecology, Community and Lifestyle*. Cambridge: Cambridge University Press, 1989.

"Should We Try to Relieve Cases of Extreme Suffering in Nature?" *PanEcology* 6, no. 1 (1991), pp. 1-5.

WORKS ABOUT OR INFLUENCED BY ARNE NAESS

This list is only a sampling, and those interested in what each of these works owes to the life and thought of Arne Naess will need to consult them firsthand. For a more complete list, see *In Sceptical Wonder: Inquiries into the Philosophies of Arne Naess on the Occasion of His 70th Birthday*, ed. Ingemund Gullvåg and Jon Wetlesen (1982). *Wisdom and the Open Air: The Norwegian Roots of Deep Ecology*, ed. Peter Reed and David Rothenberg, presents the range of Norway's environmental thought and its connection to the inspiration of Naess. Also scan the pages of *Inquiry*, a journal of interdisciplinary thought founded by Naess in the sixties. There is, of course, much more criticism of Naess's earlier philosophical forays in the Scandinavian languages. A bibliography of these is available from Universitetsforlaget, Oslo.

Abbey, Edward. *Hayduke Lives!* Boston: Little, Brown, 1990.
Bookchin, Murray. "Social Ecology vs. Deep Ecology: A Challenge for the Ecology Movement." *Green Perspectives*, no. 4 (1987), pp. 1-23.
Bookchin, Murray, and Dave Foreman. *Defending the Earth: A Dialog.* Boston: South End Press, 1991.
Bradford, George. "How Deep Is Deep Ecology?" *Fifth Estate*, Fall 1987, pp. 5-30.
Cheney, Jim. "The Neo-Stoicism of Radical Environmentalism." *Environmental Ethics* 11 (1989), pp. 293-325.
Devall, Bill. *Simple in Means, Rich in Ends.* Salt Lake City, Utah: Peregrine Smith Books, 1987.
Devall, Bill, and George Sessions. *Deep Ecology: Living As If Nature Mattered.* Salt Lake City, Utah: Peregrine Smith Books, 1985.

Drengson, Alan. *Beyond Environmental Crisis: From Technocrat to Planetary Person*. New York: Peter Lang, 1990.

Ehrenfeld, David. *The Arrogance of Humanism*. New York: Oxford University Press, 1978.

Feyerabend, Paul. *Against Method*. New York: Verso, 1988.

Fox, Warwick. "Deep Ecology: A New Philosophy for Our Time?" *Ecologist* 14, no. 5/6 (1984), pp. 194-200.

_____ . *Toward a Transpersonal Ecology: Developing New Foundations for Environmentalism*. Boston: Shambhala, 1990.

Galtung, Johan. *Methodology and Ideology*. Copenhagen: Chr. Ejlers Forlag, 1977.

Grey, William. "A Critique of Deep Ecology." *Journal of Applied Philosophy* 3 (1986), pp. 211-16.

Guha, Ramachandra. "Radical American Environmentalism and Wilderness Preservation: A Third World Critique." *Environmental Ethics* 11 (1989), pp. 71-83.

Gullvåg, Ingemund. "Naess' Pluralistic Metaphilosophy." *Inquiry* 18 (1975), pp. 391-408.

_____ . "Depth of Intention." *Inquiry* 26 (1983), pp. 31-83.

Gullvåg, Ingemund, and Jon Wetlesen, eds. *In Sceptical Wonder: Inquiries into the Philosophies of Arne Naess on the Occasion of His 70th Birthday*. Oslo: Universitetsforlaget, 1982. [Contains articles on Naess's work by Fons Elders, Johan Galtung, Harald Ofstad, Knut Erik Tranøy, Siri Naess, Ragnar Naess, Geir Hestmark, Nils Roll-Hansen, Audun Øfsti, Stein Bråten, Hans Skjervheim, Alastair Hannay, Einar Jahr, and the editors.]

Kvaløy, Sigmund. "Ecophilosophy and Ecopolitics: Thinking and Acting in Response to the Threats of Ecocatastrophe." *North American Review* 259, no. 2 (1974), pp. 16-28.

LaChapelle, Dolores. *Sacred Land, Sacred Sex: Rapture of the Deep*. Silverton, Colo.: Finn Hill Arts, 1989.

Latour, Bruno. *Science in Action*. Cambridge, Mass.: Harvard University Press, 1987.

Mathews, Freya. *The Ecological Self*. New York: Routledge, 1991.

McKeon, Richard, and Stein Rokkan. *Democracy in a World of Tensions*. Chicago: University of Chicago Press, 1951.

Meeker, Joseph. *The Comedy of Survival*. New York: Charles Scribner, 1974.

Milbrath, Lester. *Environmentalists: Vanguard for a New Society*. Albany, N.Y.: SUNY Press, 1984.

Norton, Bryan. *Why Preserve Natural Variety?* Princeton, N.J.: Princeton University Press, 1987.

Oelschlaeger, Max. *The Idea of Wilderness.* New Haven, Conn.: Yale University Press, 1991.

Ofstad, Harald. "Objectivity of Norms and Value-Judgments according to Recent Scandinavian Philosophy." *Philosophy and Phenomenological Research* 12 (1951), pp. 42-68.

Quine, W. V. O. *Word and Object.* Cambridge, Mass.: Harvard University Press, 1960.

Reed, Peter. "Man Apart: An Alternative to the Self-Realization Approach as a Basis for an Environmental Ethic." *Environmental Ethics* 11 (1989), pp. 53-69.

———, and David Rothenberg, eds. *Wisdom in the Open Air: The Norwegian Roots of Deep Ecology.* Minneapolis: University of Minnesota Press, 1992.

Rodman, John. "The Dolphin Papers." *North American Review* (1974). Reprinted in *On Nature*, ed. Daniel Halpern. Berkeley: North Point Press, 1989, pp. 252-80.

Rothenberg, David. "A Platform of Deep Ecology." *Environmentalist* 7 (1987), pp. 185-90.

———. *Hand's End: Technology and the Limits of Nature.* Berkeley: University of California Press, 1993, forthcoming.

Sessions, George. "Shallow and Deep Ecology: A Review of the Literature." In *Ecological Consciousness*, ed. Robert Schultz and Donald Hughes. Lanham, Md.: University Press of America, 1981.

Soulé, Michael. "What Is Conservation Biology?" *BioScience* 35, no. 11 (1985), pp. 727-34.

Sylvan, Richard. "A Critique of Deep Ecology." *Radical Philosophy* 40 (1985), pp. 2-12.

Taylor, Paul. *Respect for Nature.* Princeton, N.J.: Princeton University Press, 1986.

Tennessen, Herman. "Knowledge versus Survival." *Inquiry* 16 (1974), pp. 407-14.

Tobias, Michael, ed. *Deep Ecology.* San Diego: Avant Books, 1985.

Watson, Richard. "Eco-Ethics: Challenging the Underlying Dogmas of Environmentalism." *Whole Earth Review*, March 1985, pp. 5-13.

Wittbecker, Alan. "Deep Anthropology: Ecology and Human Order." *Environmental Ethics* 8 (1986), pp. 261-70.

Worster, Donald. *Nature's Economy.* Cambridge: Cambridge University Press, 1985.

Zapffe, Peter Wessel. *Den Fortapte Sønn* (The prodigal son). Oslo, 1951.

———. *Om det Tragiske* (On the tragic). 1941. Reprint. Oslo: Aventura Forlag, 1986.

Zimmerman, Michael. "Feminism, Deep Ecology, and Environmental Ethics." *Environmental Ethics* 9 (1987), pp. 21-44.

Zinkernagel, P. "Scepticism and Conditions for Description." *Inquiry* 11 (1969), pp. 190-204.

INDEX

David Rothenberg is assistant professor of humanities at the New Jersey Institute of Technology. He has degrees from Boston and Harvard universities. He spent several years at the University of Oslo, collaborating with Arne Naess on *Ecology, Community and Lifestyle*, and has worked for the British magazine, *The Ecologist*. He is also a composer and jazz clarinetist, and his music has been heard at Tanglewood and the BAM Next Wave Festival.